THE ĀCĀRYA

Śaṅkara of Kālaḍī

THE ĀCĀRYA

Śaṅkara of Kāladī

A STORY

I. S. Madugula

MOTILAL BANARSIDASS PUBLISHERS
PRIVATE LIMITED • DELHI

Reprint : Delhi, 2006
Second Revised Edition: Delhi, 2001
Reprint Edition: Delhi, 1991
First Edition: Delhi, 1985

ISBN: 81-208-0009-5 (Cloth)
ISBN: 81-208-1802-4 (Paper)

MOTILAL BANARSIDASS
41 U.A. Bungalow Road, Jawahar Nagar, Delhi 110 007
8 Mahalaxmi Chamber, 22 Bhulabhai Desai Road, Mumbai 400 026
236, 9th Main III Block, Jayanagar, Bangalore 560 011
203 Royapettah High Road, Mylapore, Chennai 600 004
Sanas Plaza, 1302 Baji Rao Road, Pune 411 002
8 Camac Street, Kolkata 700 017
Ashok Rajpath, Patna 800 004
Chowk, Varanasi 221 001

Printed in India
BY JAINENDRA PRAKASH JAIN AT SHRI JAINENDRA PRESS,
A-45 NARAINA, PHASE-I, NEW DELHI 110 028
AND PUBLISHED BY NARENDRA PRAKASH JAIN FOR
MOTILAL BANARSIDASS PUBLISHERS PRIVATE LIMITED,
BUNGALOW ROAD, DELHI 110 007

To the Memory

of

My Ācārya,

Professor K. R. Srinivasa Iyengar,

Respectfully.

INTRODUCTION

I WOULD LIKE to consider the following story of Śaṅkara a meditation on his relevance for mankind, and that makes this brief introduction a sort of pre-meditation. But, since meditation is usually unpremeditated, an introduction may be superfluous, except as a time-honored convention. In that spirit, let me share a few thoughts with you as I try to understand the phenomenon that is Śaṅkara.

There is hardly anything new in the story itself. It is just told in a new way, the imagined way of a devoted disciple, a disciple who was in every way as great as the master himself and one in whose abilities the master had the utmost confidence. The narrator of the story could as well be Sureśvara or Toṭaka or Hastāmalaka, for they were all equally great, but it seemed to me that Padmapāda had a slight edge over them. He came to the Ācārya first and thus spent the longest time with him. He seems to have a certain personal rapport with his teacher that the others may not exactly match. Sureśvara was a scholar; Toṭaka was a devoted personal attendant; Hastāmalaka was an ascetic. There may not have existed the same degree of intellectual and human symbiosis between them and the master as between Padmapāda and the master. Padmapāda then is the most plausible narrator of the master's life story. Remember, though, that we are only talking about plausibility. Padmapāda never wrote a biography of Śaṅkara.

A writer is under some obligation to justify his work to his readers. Why retell the story of Śaṅkara the details of which anyone who is even remotely interested in the *advaita* philosophy is familiar with? The answer is that custom does not diminish the majesty of his life nor does it stale the tantalizing profundity of his teachings. In fact, there is a paradox, one to which the most other-worldly of saints is subject, in the short but glorious life of Śaṅkara. He was an uncompromising non-dualist who boldly declared that there is only one Reality, everything else and everyone else being only reflections thereof if they are real at all, yet he visited all the major temples of the time and composed hymns to the deities enshrined in them. He was a saint, yet the most human of human beings. He loved his mother as no other son could ever do. He had no family of his own, yet he looked after his students with greater affection than any parent could. He constantly lived in universal consciousness, yet he tried to alleviate the misery of ordinary people with every breath of his life. The world's greatest persons live and work for others. So did Śaṅkara. Put simply, Śaṅkara was at once the best of humans, the divinest of saints, and the greatest of teachers. He desired nothing for himself, yet he was prepared to offer his life to those who wanted it.

There is a more selfish reason why I wanted to retell the Śaṅkara story. I wanted to hear it myself once again. I was aware that I could not improve upon the previous biographers if I tried to. In fact, I depended upon them for my source material, the foremost among them being the very faithful translation of Vidyāraṇya's work by the Ramakrishna Mission. I selected a few specific incidents and highlighted them as being indicative of the personality of the protagonist. I strung the episodes into a story, keeping in mind the requirement that a story should hold reader interest from start to finish. The events should contribute to the progress of the story, regardless of how different readers interpret them.

Additionally, I have interlaced the events with the principal elements of the master's teachings. I believe that they are of immediate interest to us all insofar as they answer the questions uppermost in our minds. We all have different philosophical concerns based on our age, background, and religious propensities. I daresay that it is precisely in this respect that this book is relevant. Several people who read the manuscript felt that the two aspects of the book, the story and the message blend harmoniously. Our age is one of serious inquiry into the secrets of nature and mind. Interestingly, so were the ages of the Buddha, Jesus, and Śaṅkara. Humankind continues to benefit from the inquiries of great minds, both religious and secular. In the case of the present work, after you have read and forgotten the story and even the "philosophy," you won't forget that you have the gift of inquiry. It reminds you that you cannot stop investigating the world around you and the worlds beyond. The natural and inescapable conclusion to this investigation is Self-realization, however distant that prospect might be, because all the worlds originate within you, the bearer of the divine spark.

What other justification does a work need for its existence?

I. S. MADUGULA

PREFACE TO THE SECOND EDITION

IN A MANNER of speaking, a second edition of *The Ācārya: Śaṅkara of Kāladī* seems to suggest itself. The first edition, and a second printing, sold out. It received a modicum of reader approbation, which gave me the necessary encouragement. Furthermore, in the decade and a half since its first publication, I have had an opportunity to mull Śaṅkara's teachings at a deeper level, and some of the results of that renewed understanding are interspersed throughout this edition. I have added an index, rewritten some text, and changed a few words here and there. I have not disturbed the main story element, so that whatever merit the first edition had in that respect is still preserved here.

Understandably, I also asked myself the question of the relevance of Śaṅkara's teachings for the new millennium. For one thing, there appears to be a resurgence of interest in religion and philosophy at the present time, as witnessed by the scores of titles published in the field each year during the past decade. The media, too, have gotten on the bandwagon, especially in the U.S. There are quite a few programs on religion and related issues on television, and several pages of announcements from religious groups in the weekend editions of newspapers. Apparently, even on the mundane level, it is profitable to be religious and spiritual.

All this heightened activity may be interpreted as a renewed curiosity about religion and what it can offer to the individual in the new millennium. It could also be a reinvestigation of the individual spirit and how far it can go in terms of its advertised capabilities. Is there a limit to those capabilities and, if so, how can one transcend those limitations? More importantly, how can one realize one's total potential, beyond the few tricks offered by popular psychology? "Be happy" is easier said than done. And how does one know what real happiness is? As we know from casual observation, the definition of happiness varies dramatically from one person to the next. While accumulation of wealth appears to make one person happy, giving it away keeps another perfectly contented. While many indulge, some abstain. Some exult in violence, others in peace. Erudition inspires some, contemplation soothes others. Everyone thus seems to enjoy what he or she is doing.

Now, if everyone is really happy, why is there so much misery in the world? For one thing, the pursuit of certain kinds of happiness by some is predicated upon the misery of others. For another, the happiness of even those who are indulging themselves seems to be tentative. The happiness of the successful burglar is the cause of the homeowner's misery. The perpetrator of violence is responsible for the misery of the victim. But the non-sadistic forms of happiness also include an element of discomfort. The taste of good food soon leads to indigestion. The so-called pleasures of the flesh are fraught with even longer-lasting discomfort, physical as well as mental, and are sought in the belief that they are worth the price. Happiness grounded in the possession of wealth is coterminous with that possession, even as security derived from members of the family hangs on the gossamer thread of their constantly fluctuating affections and loyalties.

Why is this so, given the fact that human nature is essentially one of happiness? All humans desire to be happy at all times, so it is safe to assume that happiness is our birthright. Ramana Maharshi (1879-1950) explains:[1]

> The desire for happiness (*sukha prema*) is a proof of the ever-existing happiness of the Self. Otherwise how can desire for it arise in you? If headache was natural to human beings no one would try to get rid of it. But everyone that has headache tries to get rid of it, because he has known a time when he had no headache. He desires only that which is natural to him. So too he desires happiness because it is natural to him. Being natural, it is not acquired.

Something strange is happening here. Our nature is happiness, we pursue happiness, yet we are not really happy, except perhaps momentarily. For the most part we keep living in actual misery or on the verge of it. We refer to this situation as the "human condition."

The greatest contribution of *advaita* to humankind is precisely the resolution of this paradox, followed by a practical course of action to eliminate all notion of misery. Starting from the bold statement that humans are meant to be not only happy but also *free*, the sages have clearly described the steps to help us return to our original glory and state of bliss and help us be all we can be.

What appears at first sight to be happiness is not real or lasting happiness, because it is "mixed with misery."[2]

> Happiness mixed with misery is only misery. When misery is eliminated then the ever-present happiness is said to be gained. Pleasure which ends in pain is misery. Man wants to eschew such pleasure.

---

[1] *Talks with Ramana Maharshi* (Tiruvannamalai: Sri Ramanasramam, 1994), p. 583 (Three volumes in one).
[2] *Ibid.*

Patañjali puts it thus:[3]

> To the discriminating, all is, as it were, painful on account of everything bringing pain either as consequence or as anticipation of loss of happiness, or as fresh craving arising from impressions of happiness, and also as counteraction of qualities.

The yogi knows that what we commonly call happiness is fraught with pain because it is something that we perceive through our mind and has no basis in reality. The mind tells us that something is pleasurable and that another is painful, both terms being merely relative.

How does the mind trick us into believing that something that is not, is? Thereby hangs a tale; in fact, the whole story. The mind is a strong organ which tries to control us at every turn. It imposes its modifications on our thinking and even intelligence. It attracts, repels, loves, hates, thinks, dreams, and wakes. Unless we watch constantly and diligently, it takes charge of all our faculties. While we believe we are dealing with "our" minds, the mind corrupts the master-servant paradigm to the point we succumb to its machinations, unless we remind ourselves that we hold the reins to our minds. The control and training of the mind and its attitudes and postures is the subject matter of yoga:[4]

---

[3] *Yogasūtra*, II, 15. *pariṇāmatāpasaṁskāraduḥkhaiḥ guṇavṛttivirodhācca duḥkhameva sarvaṁ vivekinaḥ.* Translated by Swami Vivekananda. *The Complete Works of Swami Vivekananda* (Calcutta: Advaita Ashrama, 1989), vol. 1, p. 246.

[4] *Ibid.*, p. 200.

> Yoga is restraining the mind-stuff (chitta) from taking various forms.

How is this rogue mind to be controlled? Through *abhyāsa* and *vairāgya*,[5] or sustained practice and non-attachment. The practice continues over a long period of time and the absence of attachment applies to any and all desire. The desire to do good, for example, is also a desire, as is the desire to be liberated. While initially such "positive" desires are permitted, the yogi or the sage eventually must get rid of them as well.

In addition to *abhyāsa* and *vairāgya*, ceaseless meditation is also recommended to control the runaway mind. The object of this meditation should be the Supreme Reality, all other objects being sublimated to it. Wherever the mind wanders, there is nothing but that Reality.[6] And there are some suggestions on the mechanics of this meditation incorporated in authorities like *Brahmasūtra* and the *Bhagavadgītā*. The meditator should be seated and motionless,[7] in a clean spot that is neither too high nor too low.[8]

Ramana Maharshi, famous for simplifying complex philosophical notions, characterizes meditation thus:[9]

---

[5] *Yogasūtra.*, I, 12. *abhyasavairāgyābhyāṁ tannirodhaḥ.*

[6] Śaṅkara. *Aparokṣānubhūtiḥ*, 122.

[7] *Brahmasūtra,* IV, i, 1. *āvṛttir asakṛd upadeśāt. Āsīnas saṁbhavāt,* IV, i, 6; *acalatvaṁcāpekṣya* , IV, I, 9.

[8] *Bhagavadgītā* VI, 11. *śucau deśepratiṣṭhāpya... nātyucchritam nāti nīcam...*

[9] *Talks with Sri Ramana Maharshi*, p. 256.

> Meditation is sticking to one thought. That single thought keeps away other thoughts; distraction of the mind is a sign of its weakness. By constant meditation it gains strength, i.e. to say, its weakness of fugitive thought gives place to the enduring background free from thoughts. This expanse devoid of thought is Self.

He added:

> Everyone says "I am the body." It is the experience of the sage as also of the ignorant. The ignorant man believes that the Self is confined to the body only, whereas the wise man believes that the body cannot remain apart from the Self. The Self is infinite for him and includes the body also.

If one is unable to practice *abhyāsa* or *vairāgya*, one has the simple choice of surrendering oneself to the Lord.[10] The surrender has to be total and unconditional and eternal. What is meant is the surrender of one's will itself. Then it is His responsibility to take care of the individual.

We have been talking at some length about the mind and its role in our spiritual evolution. It is necessary to do so because, deficient and detrimental as it is in terms of spiritual progress, it is all we have to take us from here to there. We can discard it totally when we reach the goal but, until then, it is all we have to work with, including its vagaries and modifications.

Why should we worry about the Self or the Spirit or *Brahman* or the Reality or Supreme Consciousness at all, in the first place? Because we have no choice. Whether we

---

[10] *Yogasūtra*, I, 23. *Īśvarapraṇidhānād vā.*

know it or not, we are all moving toward the Self, the soul of all beings, and the *source* of all beings.[11]

And Vedanta is the science that investigates that Self This investigation has been carried out by the ancients, and in modern times notably by Ramakrishna Paramahamsa and Ramana Maharshi. Both of these great souls who lived among ordinary people have provided us with an independent confirmation of the Vedanta philosophy as expounded by the master, Śaṅkara. Neither of them set out to test Śaṅkara's philosophy as such, but ended up agreeing with him as a result of their personal investigations and practices. Also, each made the path to freedom, i.e. freedom from the bondage of all the traps that the mind sets for us and the distractions that it sends our way *via* the senses, clear to us. Vedanta is the great empirical science that enabled Ramakrishna to boldly and unhesitatingly declare, "Yes, I have seen God," when someone pointedly asked him about his experience. Ramana Maharshi authoritatively equated his own self with the Universal Self and proclaimed the unity of all selves as partaking of that Self. While psychobiology today grapples with the notions of the mind and consciousness, the Aryans controlled the former and tasted the latter in its purest form as they meditated on the banks of the Gaṅgā and its tributaries millennia ago.

Śaṅkara proclaimed that *Brahman* or the Self is the one Reality, described in many different ways. Each one of us

---

[11] *Brahmasūtra*, I, i, 2. *janmādyasya yataḥ*. (Brahman is that from which the universe is born, and also which sustains and destroys it, by semantic extension.)

is part of that Self and hence free by nature. The world as we know it is nothing but a dream, a projection on the screen of the Self. While undoubtedly it exists for ordinary people, it is non-existent and inconsequential to the liberated person. To become liberated and start enjoying Universal Bliss, all we need to do is to get rid of the intrusive mind. Surely, in deep sleep, we already enjoy this Bliss. When we see a beautiful sight or hear a haunting melody, we are reminded of our blissful nature, at which moment nothing else exists in the world for us.[12]

In the teachings of Ramana Maharshi, we are told that the easiest and most direct way to realize oneself for any person regardless of gender, age, religion, creed, or any other superficially differentiating characteristic, is for one to ask oneself the basic question, "Who am I?" This is the least controversial starting point because one believes in one's own existence if nothing else. One doesn't even have to think to know that one exists because, there must be a thinker to conduct the act of thinking in the first place. So the famous Cartesian dictum, "Cogito, ergo sum," would appear to put the cart before the horse. And one exists through all the states of consciousness—waking, sleeping, and dreaming. As this self-inquiry progresses, one realizes that one is indeed the true self, the Self of all, the *summum bonum*, and the substratum not just of humankind but of all existence.[13]

---

[12] Kālidāsa. *Abhijñānaśākuntalam*, V. 2. *ramyāṇi vīkṣya madhurāṇiśca niśamya śabdān paryutsuko bhavati yat sukhito 'pi jantuḥ.*

[13] *The Teachings of Bhagavan Sri Ramana Maharshi in His Own Words* (Tiruvannamalai: Sri Ramanasramam, 1996), p. 137.

> Ask yourself the question. The body...and its functions are not 'I.' Going deeper, the mind...and its functions are not 'I.' The next step takes one to the question: Wherefrom do these thoughts arise? The thoughts may be spontaneous, superficial, or analytical. They operate on the mind. Then who is aware of them? The existence of thoughts, their clear conception and operation, become evident to the individual. This analysis leads to the conclusion that the individual is operative as the cogniser of the existence of thoughts and their sequence. This individuality is the ego, or, as people say, 'I'...Inquiring further, the questions arise: What is this 'I?' Wherefrom does it come? 'I' was not aware in sleep. Simultaneously with its rise, sleep changes to dream and wakefulness. But I am not concerned with the dream state just now. Who am I now, in the wakeful state? If I originated on waking from sleep, then the 'I' was covered up with ignorance. Such an ignorant 'I' cannot be what the scriptures refer to or the wise affirm. 'I' am beyond even sleep; 'I' must be here and now, and must be what I was all along in sleep and dream also, unaffected by the qualities of these states. 'I' must therefore be the unqualified substratum underlying these three states.

It is further explained that seeking the source of "I" helps one to eschew all other thoughts and takes one to the Self who is the seer and doer of everything, the Architect of all that is seen and beyond. The nature of the mind, where all thoughts arise, vis-à-vis the Self where all thought disappears, is elucidated thus:[14]

[14] *The Teachings*, p. 141-2.

> The mind is merely thoughts. Of all thoughts the thought 'I' is the root. Therefore, the mind is only the thought 'I.' Whence does this thought 'I' arise? Seek for it within; it then vanishes. This is the pursuit of the Wisdom. Where the 'I' vanishes, there appears 'I'—'I' by itself. This is the Infinite...The state non-emergence of 'I' is the state of being THAT.

"THAT" of course is one's true state, which can be attained only after the false 'I' or ego disappears. Although it reveals itself as 'I,' it is not the ego but the perfect being, the Absolute Self.

When someone asked Ramana Maharshi how to practice this kind of self-inquiry while one is employed professionally, he said:[15]

> There will be no conflict. As you practice both and develop your powers you will be able to attend to both. You will begin to look on business as a dream.

Such are the comprehensive, universal conceptions of Vedanta as reformulated by Śaṅkara and reaffirmed in their own lives by Ramakrishna Paramahamsa and his disciple, Vivekananda, and Ramana Maharshi. There are no dogmas, no beliefs, no superstitions, but just the proven basics and facts. There is not even any reference to a "religion" as the term is commonly understood today. Belong to a religion if you must, but find out who you are for yourself. You can analyze your own psyche better than any psychiatrist can, if you know how to go about it.

In light of the above, the question how Śaṅkara is relevant to the new millennium is almost redundant. The truths that he expounded are millennia-old and valid for all

---

[15] *Talks*, p. 39

millennia to come. If however one were to enumerate the chief tenets preached and practiced by him, they would be:

- You are that Self that permeates all existence, and part of that divinity that indwells all creation.
- To realize your true nature, you will have to inquire into yourself and ask yourself, "Who am I?" By a process of regression and by understanding what you are not (e.g. I am not the body, I am not the mind), you will arrive at your Self, where all analysis ends.
- Though your true nature is Bliss, your mind makes you believe that you are unhappy through association with painful events. But since pleasure and pain are the two sides of the same coin, avoid both.
- Look upon all creation as the work of the Almighty, whose heir you are. You are that same Energy, same Consciousness, same Spirit.
- Do your work without the thought of reward. You will get what is coming to you. You are not the doer, though it might appear to be so. You are only the observer. This makes any work easier and even enjoyable for you.[16]

---

[16] *Talks*, p. 599. "The Gita starts saying that you are not the body, that you are not therefore the *karta*... That one should act without thinking that oneself is the actor. The actions go on despite his egolessness. The person has come into this manifestation for a certain purpose. That purpose will be accomplished whether one considers himself the actor or not."

- Work is not a hindrance to meditation, and neither is family. Set aside a few minutes a day to be alone and delve into yourself.
- Mental modifications such as stress and depression only flourish if you let them. Get rid of the mind that makes you think that you are depressed or stressed. Banish the thoughts and you are whole once again.
- Reform yourself before you reform the world. Be aware that you are free, liberated, and blissful to begin with. The only obstacle to freedom is the thought that you are not free. Don't think, just be, and you are truly happy.

The greatest feature of the "religion" of the Vedas, if it can be called a religion, is that it is so comprehensive that all formal religions appear be subsumed by it. It affirms unequivocally that humankind is free, that it is divine, that it is blissful.

And we are indebted to Śaṅkara for making that clear to us.

Palm Springs, California I. S. MADUGULA
Sankranti, 2001

TABLE OF CONTENTS

PROLOGUE

In the beginning there was Silence. The Silence was utterly aware of itself. Utterly potent. Utterly conscious. Being formless, it imagined itself to be a form. The formless form was *Puruṣa*, the Person. The Person looked around and found Itself filling the four quarters. The Person slept and dreamed of Itself. The Person looked within and recognized itself. Because the Silence totally pervaded the *Puruṣa*, it was Its Self. Because it was omnipresent, it was *Brahman.* Because it was omnipotent, it was the Word.

Eons later, the Person wished to see many selves emanate from Itself. Out of the Silence, which was Its own Self, It fashioned the primal Substance and let it be. Out of the Substance arose Earth and Heaven, the sun and the stars, hills and dales, rivers and seas, bird and beast, and humans and all manner of creatures. And the Silence was peopled.

More eons later, the creatures lost sight of the bond between themselves and *Puruṣa*. Between their selves and the Self. They forgot that the Self was *Brahman*. And that they were *Brahman* They needed a guide, a teacher. A teacher who could show them again who they were, a teacher *extraordinaire*, a teacher of god and human, a *jagad guru*. Such a teacher was Śaṅkara, the bestower of Bliss.

SANANDANA MEETS THE ĀCĀRYA

It was like yesterday. I remember it all distinctly. Twenty summers only sharpen my memory of that glorious spring day when I first saw your radiant face and, without a second thought, surrendered myself at your feet. Reflected in the serene waters of the Maṇikarṇikā Ghāṭ, it was as if the sunny sheen of the face made the lotuses of the feet bloom. The swans floating down the Gaṅgā were fooled, for there were no lotus stalks to feed on. Just the flowers. They ducked in the water and the flowers disappeared, further confounding them. It was a magnificent sight. The spires of a thousand temples to one side and the endless sea of flaming water to the other. And the golden dome of the abode of Viśvanātha towering over them all. Holy thoughts filled the hearts of swami and sinner alike, and the minds were glad to turn within.

None could of course celebrate the soul-stirring beauty and greatness of Kāśī as well as you did. The city rivaled the splendor of the world of Indra, the lord of gods. The difference however was that Kāśī was the gateway to liberation from human bondage. It provided a means of escape from the human condition. Indra could not offer his subjects freedom from the bonds of pleasure. You pointed out, moreover, in a beautiful verse that Kāśī really was the inmost being of us all and that the Gaṅgā was the eternally pure stream of knowledge. People therefore are doubly drawn to Kāśī. As long as they live there, they are in touch with themselves. When they die, they are released from the cyclical return to life, from *saṁsāra*. Your words are vibrant with music:

kāśyāmitu kāśate kāśī
kāśī sarvaprakāśikā
sā kāśī viditā yena
tena prāptā hi kāśikā

As a boy from the Cola country in the south, I received my early training in the four Vedas and the related sciences. But the emptiness of book learning troubled me. I knew that true wisdom could be gained only from a self-realized guru who lived that wisdom every minute of his life. I came across many teachers whose secondhand knowledge failed to impress me. My searches brought me to Kāśī, the ageless seat of art and science, dharma and renunciation. And there you were, the embodiment of my good fortune, the ācārya of ācāryas. Your questions were probing, but your voice was comforting.

"Who are you?"

"I come from afar, where flows the great Kāverī, kindling true faith and devotion in the hearts of people. I am a brahmin by birth and a seeker of spiritual enlightenment. I am alone, unattached. They call me Sanandana."

"But who *are* you?

"That, O Great Ācārya, is what I would like to find out with the help of your instruction and by your grace. I hope I qualify for both. I have this conviction that this life is worthless as it is full of ignorance and delusion which in turn generate the evil passions of lust, greed, and envy. I have no taste for sensual pleasures which lead one into the quagmire of desire. The only desire I have is to serve you and in your company to enjoy the ultimate bliss which is beyond words.

"Occasionally, as I sit by myself or watch the clouds pass overhead in their ethereal majesty or observe the chicks crack open their way into the world, I am overwhelmed by certain intangible feelings. I feel that I am a part of everything and everything is part of me. I do not know. I cannot understand any of it. Am I or am I not limited by my body? Or my mind? Or intellect? Why do I feel so powerful yet so helpless? So happy yet so wretched? What is the meaning of life? O Merciful One, please deign to instruct me in true knowledge. You will not find me ungrateful or unworthy of your kindness. I beg you to remember that people call you Śaṅkara, the provider of comfort and dispeller of ignorance."

The gracious smile on your lips indicated that you were pleased with my supplication. You looked into my eyes and my heart intently for a full minute, ignoring everyone else, and through silence initiated me into the life of a monk and the study of the Self. It was as if you meant to say, "You are not Sanandana or the brahmin boy from the banks of the Kāverī or a Vedic scholar. You are not the senses nor mind nor body. You are *you*. You are *That*—which alone matters. You are the consciousness pervading all. You are not affected by virtue or vice, joy or sorrow, heat or cold, mantra or tantra. You have no caste or creed, father or mother, birth or death. No friends, no relatives, not even a guru. You are the quintessence of awareness."

That was the beginning of my real existence. Never once did I leave your side thereafter as long as you chose to bless this world in your body. You were the substance, and I was the shadow. Now all I can do is recount those wonderful times spent in your divine presence. People say that your advent into this world was itself a legend, that you were a born ācārya. How often did I wish that you had been with us longer! I should perhaps not grieve over the disappearance of your physical form, if I had learnt my lessons right. But I know that you will forgive me an occasional lapse into the human plane, seeing that you were the most human of us all.

2

BIRTH OF ŚAṄKARA IN KĀLADĪ

That small village in Kerala was among the serenest in the country. Embraced lovingly by the plentiful Pūrṇā which fed its fields and nursed its gardens, Kāladī never knew the pangs of hunger or thirst. Some benevolent deity, pleased with the prayers of the brahmins and the rightful discharge of the prescribed duties by the others, extended a protective arm over the village. The rich helped the needy, the strong aided the weak. The son respected his father, and he his father, and all three lived under the same roof. Everyone did his job for the sake of all others, for he and the community were the same. Happiness was their common goal. It was also their common achievement. King Rājaśekhara was proud of this unique village in his realm. He often visited it and was known to be alike the friend of the commoner and the nobleman, the brahmin and the peasant, the ascetic and the householder.

Among the most renowned residents of the village was the brahmin Vidyādhirāja, who excelled all others in learning and piety. Though he was averse to the life of a married man, because of his desire for a son who would perform the daily *homa* and sacrificial rites, he became a householder. And a son, Śivaguru, was born to him in due course. One virtuous son, they say, is enough to redeem ten generations of forefathers from damnation. In saintliness Śivaguru was like Lord Śiva; in learning, he was like the preceptor of gods.

At the *āśrama* of his teacher, the boy Śivaguru performed his duties with great care and devotion. A remarkable fact about him was that he early showed interest in the *meaning* and import of the Vedas which were normally studied for their magical sounds and mantric potential. But those who recite the Vedas ignorant of their onerous import are likened to donkeys that carry sandalwood on their backs without in the least being aware of its fragrance. So he mastered the Vedic hymns together with their denotations and connotations. Then it was time for him to return home to his parents, but he seemed to be in no hurry to do so. The teacher called him one day to his side and told him, "My child, you have now completed your studies and you know all that I know. You must now go home and join your relatives who will be eager to see you. Also, custom dictates that boys get married after they finish their education. That is the proper time for them to do so. Your father must already be planning your marriage."

To this the boy replied, "Revered Sir, what you say about the Vedic path of life is only partly true, for the Vedas also declare that if a *brahmacārin*, at the completion of his studies, desires to become a *sannyāsin*, he may do so. I am desirous of renouncing *samsāra* so that I can continue in your school for life chanting the Veda. There is nothing greater in this life than service to one's guru who is the conferer of enlightenment. The worldly state of matrimony is not for me. Everyone knows that marriage looks attractive for a short period, and the troubles thereafter are endless. A married man needs money to support his family and entertain guests. With increasing responsibility comes the need for more money, and there is no end to his wants. After a great deal of trouble and expense, he performs a ritual, but he is not sure that he has done it properly. The wrong performance of sacrifice can be very harmful. So please do not send me off to get married."

As Śivaguru's teacher was wondering how to convince his young disciple, Vidyādhirāja arrived at the *āśrama* to take the boy home. It was now his father's turn to persuade him, which he was able to do after considerable effort. Śivaguru's mother and the large number of relatives who gathered at home welcomed him heartily. The mother was beside herself with joy and would not tire of talking about how grown and how learned her little boy was. Vidyādhirāja for his part wanted to test the boy's learning by asking him intricate questions on philosophy and literature. He was quickly convinced that his son was not only well-mannered but also scholarly.

As word about Śivaguru's return home spread, fathers of girls flocked to Vidyādhirāja's house offering their daughters in marriage to Śivaguru together with promises of a handsome dowry in cash and kind. The noble brahmin selected a suitable bride with good looks and pleasant disposition and told her father, Māgha Paṇḍita, that the wedding would take place on condition that the girl would not bring any dowry with her. This violation of the custom surprised and pleased Māgha Paṇḍita, and Śivaguru married Āryā in a solemn ceremony. The newlyweds were suited to each other like the night and the moon. Poets sang that if Śivaguru was the cloud, Āryā was the lightning; if he was the tree, she was the vine that entwined it; if he was the flower, she was the fragrance.

In the company of Āryā, Śivaguru meticulously performed the daily rites enjoined on householders. They visited many shrines and bathed in sacred waters. Once they were resting in the Śiva temple in Trichur, not far from Kāladī. They were fasting on that auspicious day and were as usual engaged in silent meditation. Then it occurred to them that, although they were happy in every respect, they had one deficiency. They did not have a child. There could be no greater curse on a householder than being childless. It must be their *prārabdha*, the result of their misdeeds in their past lives. Only Lord Śiva could take pity on them and grant them a child. And it was well known that the Lord was easily pleased by genuine devotion. Since these thoughts occurred to both of them at the same time, there was no need for Śivaguru to discuss the matter with his wife. Despite his knowledge and enlightenment, Śivaguru as a family man felt the lack of offspring to be an obstacle to his salvation. He decided to extend his fast by two more days. Living only on fruit and water and observing severe chastity, he prayed to the merciful Śiva with all his heart.

On the third night, Śivaguru was quite exhausted. A little distance away in the great hall of the temple Āryā was fast asleep. He was in a state of consciousness between waking and sleep. Then he felt that, amidst a sea of bright light, Śiva spoke to him in a soothing voice, "Śivaguru, I am pleased with your austerities, and I know the object of your prayers. I am going to give you a choice: Would you like a distinguished but short-lived son or a mediocre one with a long span of life?"

Śivaguru had no hesitation. He chose the former. The father always feels happy when his son is highly regarded by the world. It is better for one to live a few years like a swan than for decades like a crow. Śivaguru's wish was granted. While he still remained in a dazed condition, he saw a ray of light traveling from the Śiva image in the inner temple toward his sleeping wife.

Without explaining how it all happened, he briefly told her that their prayers were answered. They returned home the next day, their minds overflowing with joy.

The effulgence of the Lord grew in Āryā's womb. It transcended its narrow confines and radiated from her entire body. She began to favor tart foods. Her movements became lazy, and she was easily tired. Even the gentle breeze from the south became too much for her, the fragrant jasmines too heavy to wear in her hair. She ate little or nothing. Often she had visions of the Lord riding His snow-white bull, with all the gods chanting His praise. Her bosom filled with the nectar of cosmic bliss, which the divine baby would soon drink.

Then the day arrived, quite different from other days. Tremendous calm filled the air over the village. Yet the river thrashed its banks with its jubilant waves repeatedly. Even though the sky was without a cloud, the peacocks in the garden danced merrily. The cuckoo sang even though it was not quite the season. The whole nature seemed filled with expectation.

They say that childbirth is like rebirth for the mother. Āryā's confinement however was characterized more by the joy of birth than by any discomfort. The baby resembled Śiva in every respect, perfect in limb and looks. The stars gathered themselves into auspicious constellations in the sky to watch the baby arrive. Śivaguru promptly offered prayers to the Lord, and distributed generous gifts among the villagers. His greatest wish was fulfilled in the grandest possible manner.

The astrologers predicted that the child would be unique, unparalleled in learning and forensic skill. They compared him to an elephant in a banana plantation in matter of destroying false religions and spurious doctrines. They said his powers would be unlimited. But when Śivaguru asked them pointedly about the child's longevity, they said evasively that customarily that prediction would be made in the child's eighth year of life. There was time for that.

Since the child brought so much happiness to the family, Śivaguru named him Śaṅkara, at the same time remembering his favorite deity. Before the year was out, the child Śaṅkara learned to stand unfalteringly on his feet. The first word he spoke was "I," the profound truth that he taught to the entire world later.

The boy Śaṅkara quickly gained proficiency in languages. He had a prodigious memory. Anything read to him once stuck in his fertile mind forever. So his teachers were very happy with him. They often made use of him to teach their slower pupils. Neither the correct intonation of the four Vedas nor the elucidation of the classics and the epics posed for him any problem, all of which he acquired within less than a year. Others struggled at them for no less than twelve years. The only explanation of this superhuman feat was that the boy was no ordinary boy. He was the Lord himself in mortal form. This extraordinary ability was sometimes inconvenient for the teachers. He would question them on the goals and value of learning and what knowledge it would produce in a person. The next question was what good that knowledge was unless it helped one to know oneself and the world for exactly what they were. The teachers had not suspected that there was any knowledge outside their books. The Vedas taught them the right way of performing rituals. The *śāstras* told them how to conduct their lives. Was there anything else to it? They wept and they laughed as things went ill or well. They yielded to desire. They knew nothing better.

The boy showed a superhuman calm at all times. When his father passed away in his third year, he did not feel like crying. What was death? Was it the end or the beginning? Beginning of what? End of what? If it was either, no amount of crying would do any good. If it was neither, there was no need for any concern at all. These matters, those who know do not talk about. Those who talk do not know.

Further instruction from more learned teachers confirmed the boy's belief that there must be more to the world than met the eye. One of the troublesome questions was who made this world and why. If it evolved on its own, what source did it evolve out of? What was the relationship of the individual to that source? He realized that he must find the answers on his own. He must discover the Great Truth for himself.

To study anything one must stay outside of it and examine it objectively. To understand the functioning of the world, one must renounce it. One must practice dispassion, be unattached. One must subject one's senses, those windows to the outside world, to severe testing and probe their operation thoroughly. That must be the goal of any intelligent person who does not want to be stuck in a groove. Such were the boy's thoughts when he returned home from his teachers at the age of seven. That was his meditation.

3

KING RĀJAŚEKHARA VISITS ŚAṄKARA

The story of the Ācārya as a boy was quite well known.

During the three years that he had gone for his studies, his aging mother was all alone. She needed help and company both of which he now cheerfully provided. He had just learnt the Upaniṣadic injunction, *mātṛdevo bhava*, look upon your mother as God. He loved her very much, anyway.

He had set for himself a daily routine. He would do everything that his mother wanted, study the Veda, perform the fire sacrifice twice, and follow the other stipulated observances. The villagers were happy to see him and talk to him. He was always very polite to them. His very looks inspired respect in the visitors, of whom there were plenty on account of his burgeoning reputation. He had not the slightest conceit when he discoursed with his fellow scholars in the neighborhood.

Now that her son had come back, the mother began to spend considerable time in spiritual practices. She would fast often, bathe several times a day, and worship the Lord for long hours. On one occasion, when the sun was particularly merciless, she wanted to take a bath in the river. She had just completed a fast. There was some distance to be covered, and the walk proved too much for the old lady. Midway between her home and the river, she collapsed on the ground and lay there utterly exhausted. When his mother did not return home after some time, the Ācārya became worried and retraced her steps to the river.

He broke down in tears when he found her lying helpless in the hot sun. He brought her home and refreshed her with cool water and fruit. The lady recovered after he fanned her gently for a while and looked at her son gratefully for all his service and affection.

The incident pained the Ācārya so much that he addressed a sincere prayer to the river deity asking her to be considerate toward his ailing mother. The deity was pleased with his request on behalf of his mother in true filial devotion. The next morning the villagers were surprised to find the river flowing in their very neighborhood, making their gardening and farming much easier. On learning that the Ācārya was their benefactor, they were very thankful to him. There was however one problem that the Ācārya's boyish enthusiasm had not foreseen which came to light during the following monsoon. The Kṛṣṇa temple which was situated in the valley was in danger of being submerged. The Ācārya quickly remedied this by moving the idol to a higher elevation and reinstalling it there with due ceremony. The beautiful temple still attracts worshippers by the thousands to Kāladī.

King Rājaśekhara, who was a scholar in his own right, had heard of the Ācārya's reputation and decided to invite him to his court for a conference. Accordingly, he dispatched an envoy bearing rich gifts on elephants, with instructions to bring the boy scholar to the palace. The envoy greeted the boy appropriately and said: "The king of Kerala is pleased to send me to meet you and offer these tokens of his regard for you. He is well known as much for his erudition as for his valor in the battlefield. He has a number of scholars adorning his court who advise him on good governance and right conduct. He is the most illustrious member of his lineage. He requests that you visit his court as soon as possible. I have brought the noblest of the royal elephants to take you. I await your answer." The envoy remained respectfully silent.

To these words of the minister the Ācārya replied, "I thank you sincerely for your trouble and the great king for thinking of me. Please present my humble salutations to him and tell him that I am unable to come to the palace and that I beg his forgiveness. I am a *brahmacārin* with certain duties to perform. I wear a deer skin and beg my food. I have to attend to the sacrificial fire and study the Vedas. The luxury of elephant rides and palaces is not for me in my stage of life. Above all, I love my mother too much to leave her alone. She needs me here. I am sorry I cannot fulfill the king's desire."

The noble king understood the Ācārya's mind. Desirous of meeting the *brahmacārin* at any cost, he came to Kāladī himself. He was delighted to see the boy's face reflecting a wisdom well beyond his years. He instinctively prostrated himself before him, forgetting that he was a great royal personage and the ruler of the region. Indeed those who desire nothing for themselves and who are forever engaged in the quest of the Self are superior even to emperors. The Ācārya received him with due honors within his means and wanted to know his pleasure.

Rājaśekhara presented him large quantities of gold and precious stones, and requested that he listen to three plays that he had written. The Ācārya carefully listened to them and was very impressed with their literary quality. When the king was about to leave, he pointed to the gold and gems and said, "Noble Ruler, I appreciate your offering these to me. But I have no use for them, seeing that I live by begging alone. Please therefore have them distributed to the poor people of the village."

The king would not have believed that such total detachment was possible if he had not seen it for himself.

4
ŚAṄKARA RENOUNCES THE WORLD

The Ācarya was very busy the following year. He had a number of students learning literature, grammar, logic, and philosophy. He had already begun to acquire reputation as a teacher. His method of instruction appealed to them all. He would let them read the text and struggle with its interpretation. Independent analysis was what he always encouraged. This spirit of inquiry the student found useful in his later life. The Ācārya also continued his rituals. Later, when he placed knowledge above action as a means of self-realization, he was speaking from personal experience of both ways of life. When relatives tried to discuss marriage, he would not hear of it saying that he was not interested in anything but service to his mother.

The young *brahmacārin's* self-discipline impressed the gods and sages as well. Once, during this time, four great *ṛṣi*s visited the Ācārya's home. Both mother and son were greatly pleased that such august personages as Upamanyu, Dadhīci, Gautama, and Agastya thought it fit to appear before them in this age of sin when mortal eyes had lost their divine vision. They entertained them appropriately and obtained from them a great deal of information about the world of the dead ancestors and about the duties of the living toward them.

At one point the Ācārya's mother could not help asking them, "Venerable Sages, your visit to our home is a blessing for us, indeed. I believe that your very sight has cleansed all our past sins. Taking advantage of your concern for us, I am making bold to ask you something. My little Śaṅkara here has now mastered all learning and is further possessed of various extraordinary qualities which almost frighten me. It seems to me that he is not an ordinary boy and therefore, out of anxiety, I would like to know what kind of future awaits him. Great people like you can easily read past, present, and future events, since you exist in eternity. Pray enlighten me on this question and set my mind at rest."

Then Agastya, acting as the spokesman of the group responded with compassion, "Gentle Lady, you remember that Śaṅkara was born to you as a result of austerities that you and your husband performed in the Śiva temple at Trichur? When Lord Śiva appeared to your husband in a vision and presented him with a choice between a worthless but long-lived son and an extraordinary, short-lived one, he chose the latter. Then Śiva Himself incarnated as your son, because He wanted to give you the best possible offspring and none was as great as Himself. Hence the boy's supernatural abilities.

"As regards his future, he cannot live among humans for more than sixteen years. However..." As the merciful but tactless Agastya was about to go on with a great deal more about the boy's future, the other sages pointed out that it was time for them to leave. But before he departed, Agastya did complete his sentence. "However, owing to special circumstances, he will have an additional sixteen years to live." As the Ācārya's mother was not aware of the conditions under which she became a mother, she was greatly saddened by this prediction.

The Ācārya tried his best to console his mother.

"Dearest mother, I don't know what you are worried about and why. The life of human beings on earth is so full of misery that they would often wish they were not born. It is compared to a silken flag torn by gusty winds. The dullest among people knows that the body is destined to drop at the appointed time. What the yogi alone knows is that in the cycle of *saṁsāra* one is born and dead again and again a million times, and plays the role of a son, father, husband, mother, or wife in unending succession. Anything like true and lasting happiness can be achieved only by transcending this *saṁsāra* through renunciation which is the gateway of self-knowledge. Mother, please permit me to embrace that state and strive to realize myself during the short time that I have."

This request from the boy was even a greater shock to the poor woman than her knowledge of his short life span. She spoke with much pain in her heart. "Don't ever speak that way. You break my old heart. Although I am aware that you are not destined to live long, yet I long to see you as a householder. Any girl would be proud to have you as her husband albeit for a short time. A woman who can have the good fortune of being the wife of a man like you will earn vast merit. So please heed my advice and make a doting old woman happy."

The Ācārya was amused by this argument. A woman's love for her son would make her inconsiderate toward all others. His mother was prepared to see some girl widowed before her prime just so she could play with her grandchildren. This was surely *māyā*, illusion, of the highest order. He knew however that no amount of logic would do him any good at that time. So he simply said that there was ample time to discuss the topic and kept silent. A further problem was that, unless his mother permitted, he could not take to *sannyāsa*, according to the rules. So he thought he would wait for a more opportune moment to press his request again.

After a few days, he happened to go to the river with his mother for his bath. He stepped into the river, and she sat on the edge of the water washing clothes. The next moment she heard the boy cry in distress, "Mother, mother, I think a crocodile has caught hold of my leg. I don't know what to do. I am trying to free myself but he won't let go of me." By now just the boy's face was visible above the water which was a light shade of red. There was nothing that the poor mother could do but beat her chest and wail loudly. "I lost my husband a few years ago and my son has been my hope since. Now it appears that fate is going to snatch that support away from me. O God, how can you be so cruel? What can I do now? I wish I could die first."

She kept looking at her struggling son as she wept piteously. The boy now spoke with some difficulty as he began to swallow water. "Mother, there may be just one way out of this. It is said in the *śāstras* that if one agrees to accept *sannyāsa* when one's life is in danger, one will be out of that danger. I think I should try that because there is no other way this crocodile is going to let go of my leg. Please permit me to renounce the world and bless me." The poor mother was in a spot. She had to say yes to her son's request under the circumstances. No sooner did she give her consent than the Ācārya said "*sannyasto 'ham,*" I have renounced, three times and his leg was freed. Then in token of having snapped his ties to the world, he snapped his sacred thread and threw it away Did the Ācārya stage-manage the whole episode? Who knows? He *had been* known to be tricky on occasion.

The Ācārya came out of the water doubly relieved. The crocodile released him and at the same time he got his much-desired relief from *saṁsāra.* He attributed it all to divine intervention. He was saved just in the nick of time. The mother, too, was happy. Though she could not any more think of grandchildren, at least her son's life was spared and she was thankful for that.

Now that the Ācārya had accomplished what he wanted, he was sorry for his mother who had been cheated out of a son's services. He turned toward her and said with much affection, "Mother, though I have renounced the world, you are still my mother and I am your son. Do not worry about who will take care of you. Our relatives who will now inherit my property will look after you. They will perform your last rites."

"Son, I am indeed happy that you could be saved through renunciation. I am old and infirm and I don't think the end is too far. All parents wish that their son should be by their deathbed and perform their obsequies and not some stranger. So do I. I want you to come to me when the end approaches and do the rites yourself. In fact, that is one of the principal duties of a son. This is how he discharges his debt to his parents who have given him life and brought him into this world."

"Dear mother, I understand, and I will obey your wishes, even though a *sannyāsin* is not authorized to perform his parents' last rites. Fulfilling your wishes is more important to me than some ancient injunction. You are like the very goddess to me. Just think of me when you are ill or when you feel the end is near, and I will be by your side at once. Have no worry at all on that count. I will myself cremate your body when you die. But let's not talk about those things at this time. I have to leave now in quest of my guru, which is the first duty of a novice *sannyāsin*. I have to explore the secrets of the Self, and put an end to all false teaching about it. Please bless me and permit me to leave."

"I bless you with all my heart, son. May God be with you wherever you go. I am worried, though, about your food and lodging in your wanderings. Who will take care of you?"

"Mother, you have so far taken good care of me. Now I am going out into the world and henceforth whoever feeds me is my mother, whoever teaches me is my father. My pupils are my children, peace my bride, and solitude my bliss. Such are the rigors of my undertaking."

The gracious lady tearfully hugged her son for one last time and reluctantly permitted him to go. The fact that her son was as great as Lord Śiva himself did not make any difference to her. He was her little Śaṅkara.

5
GOVINDAPĀDA ACCEPTS ŚAṄKARA

The Ācārya was barely eight years old—in fact, he would not be an Ācārya for another four years—when he became a *sannyāsin* under dire circumstances. Of course he had always wanted to be a *sannyāsin* but, now that he had actually donned the ochre robes, he had to follow a different set of rules than the one he was used to. He had to carry a staff and a small supply of water in a *kamaṇḍalu*. He should cover any distance only on foot. He should not stay at any one place for a long time, lest he should develop an attachment to it.

But the most important of all requirements was that he find for himself an enlightened guru, different from the previous teachers. Until he had completed his formal study with him, he would not be eligible to impart instruction to others. In the case of the Ācārya there was no need for this formality, but the formality had to be fulfilled.

So the young boy started in quest of a spiritual preceptor. He did not know where to find one or what he would look like. He walked relentlessly day after day, begging his food during the day and sleeping under the trees at night. At one time he was walking in open country when the sun got too hot. He decided to rest under a rock where there was some shade when a curious thing happened. There were a few frogs on the nearby ledge enjoying themselves in the ample shade of the outstretched hood of a king cobra. He remembered what the *śāstras* said: such peaceful coexistence between natural enemies was possible only in the vicinity of a great sage. On inquiry he found that there had indeed lived a great sage called Ṛṣyaśṛṅga in the neighborhood many hundreds of years ago and the peace still prevailed. The boy made a mental note of the place and proceeded on his journey. After what must have been many months and several hundred miles, he reached the banks of the mighty Narmadā.

It somehow seemed to him that his quest had ended. He had heard that the pilgrim center of Oṁkāranātha where he had reached now was the abode of many great yogis and enlightened souls, and maybe one of them could help him. Anyway, he rested there for some time enjoying the cool breeze until the ferocity of the sun had abated. Then he began making inquiries about any great guru that the residents might know of. None could help, though all were struck by the boy's earnestness. He then made his way to the temple for further search. There he met a group of travelers who did hear about a certain Govindapāda, a self-realized sage, who lived in a nearby cave. As he reached the cave, the sun was just setting, and he knew he had arrived.

The cave in which Govindapāda lived was very small with only a cubit-wide opening as its entrance. No one ever saw the sage enter or leave the cave, let alone talk to anyone. A number of other ascetics and pilgrims wanted to have an audience with the sage and pay their respects to him, but that was clearly out of the question. The sage did not desire to see anyone. The young Ācārya did not know what to do. However, as was the custom, he went round the cave three times as a mark of respect for the sage inside. Then prostrating himself at the narrow entrance, he chanted a delightful hymn in praise of the exalted guru in an attitude of fervent adoration.

"My obeisances to you, O Revered Govindapāda, who are the incarnation of the archpreceptor, Ādiśeṣa, the most ancient thousand-hooded serpent. Your fame has spread far and wide in the outside world, because you have traveled into your innermost being. You are the most realized person on earth, since you had the good fortune of being instructed in Brahman knowledge by no less a personage than the great Gauḍapāda, the famed commentator of the *Māṇḍūkya Upaniṣad,* and the founder of the non-dualistic philosophy. That Gauḍapāda was a disciple of Śuka, the son of Vyāsa, the compiler of the Vedas and the author of the *Brahmasūtra*. The immortal Vyāsa was the son Parāśara, the foremost among the lawgivers. Thus, O Govindapāda, you come from a most remarkable line of teachers. Please accept this unworthy little *sannyāsin* as your disciple and make him heir to that Brahman knowledge which the gods themselves are eager to acquire."

Govindapāda, who had been in a state of consciousness beyond waking, dream, and deep sleep, was able to hear only a part of the Ācārya's hymn, but what little he had heard was enough to impress him. He knew that here was a boy of a very high caliber. He decided to find out who he was.

"Who are you, my child?"

The question elicited a response of the rarest kind from the Ācārya, grand alike in conception and expression. It also confirmed the guru's suspicion that the fledgling *sannyāsin* was no mere beginner in spiritual practice.

"Revered Sir, I am not the earth, water, sky, fire, air, or an aggregate of these elements. Nor do I share any of their properties. I am verily Śiva, the Unified Consciousness, the One that is pure and absolute. I am beyond caste and its regimen, beyond yoga and its practices; I am the one and only Awareness that we all experience in dreamless sleep."

He continued his spontaneous composition of resonant verses:

na mātā pitā vā, na devā na lokāḥ
na vedā na yajñā, na tīrtham bruvanti.

"I cannot be identified with a father or mother, gods, worlds, or the Vedas, sacrifices or shrines. I am neither existence nor nonexistence. I am the one and only Śiva, the Absolute.

na sāṁkhyaṁ na śaivaṁ na tat pāñcarātram
na jainaṁ na mīmāṁsakāder matam vā.

"I have nothing to do with the philsophical systems of Sāṁkhya, Śaiva, Jaina, Pāñcarātra, or Mīmāṁsā.

na cordhvaṁ na cādho, na cāntar na bāhyam
na madhyaṁ na tiryaṅ, na pūrvā parā dik.

"It cannot be said that I am above or below, inside or outside; neither am I the middle or the sides, east or west. Because of my all-pervasiveness, I am the indivisible and auspicious Śiva.

na śuklaṁ na kṛṣṇaṁ, na raktaṁ na pītam
na kubjaṁ na pīnaṁ, na hrasvaṁ na dīrgham.

"My complexion is neither white, black, red, nor yellow. I am neither short nor tall, neither bent nor straight. I am the essence of light which is formless.

na śāstā na śāstraṁ, na śiṣyo na śikṣā
na ca tvaṁ na cāhaṁ, na cāyaṁ prapañcaḥ.

"My true nature cannot think of a teacher or scripture, pupil or instruction, you or I, or the phenomenal world.

"I am of the nature of the Self different from all that we see, feel, or experience. Therefore, Revered Govinda, how can I answer your question with a single name or description?"

The venerable sage was now totally convinced of the boy's uniqueness because he gave the only correct answer to his question. The ten verses recited extempore by the Ācārya have since formed the basis of the *advaita* doctrine and are repeated by students of that school everyday before the start of their lessons.

"Child, I am very pleased with your answer. I suspect that you are a great soul in human form come to earth to accomplish some mission that would be beneficial to humankind. I have therefore decided to accept you as my disciple and help you in the furtherance of that mission."

With these words the aged guru extended his feet outside the cave. The young aspirant worshipped them, thereby establishing an eternal bond with the guru. The guru, in turn, showered his affection on the most deserving disciple he ever had. He then imparted to him that most secret Brahman knowledge, that most profound wisdom which is enshrined in these four Supreme Utterances:

prajñānaṁ brahma. Brahman is Pure Consciousness.
ayamātmā brahma. This ātman is Brahman.
tat tvaṁ asi. You are That.
ahaṁ brahmāsmi. I am Brahman.

It took approximately the space of a year to cover the import of each of these declarations. In addition, the Ācārya studied the *Brahmasūtra* as a sort of culmination of the course in self-realization.

* * * * * * *

Properly instructed by the guru in the technique of the cultivation of the Self, the Ācārya was meditating on the edge of the river one monsoon day. It had been raining for a few days, but on that day the storm was particularly intense. The skies were covered with thick layers of dark clouds which presently let go of their contents. Soon drizzle changed to downpour. It was as if visible lines of communication had been established between heaven and earth. And then the gale blew in, blending the raindrops into streams before they reached the ground. There was a river gushing below, and a river gushing from above, the joint force proving too much for the river banks. The lashing winds had already felled many a tree in their path. The dwellings of the common folk were reduced to so much rubble and straw. A deafening roar pervaded the air. The flashes of lightning made nature look much darker than it was. Trees and tenements flattened by the rain and the wind were now being carried away by the flood which was like the bellowing ocean on a full-moon night. To the pandemonium were added the heart-rending cries of the people who lost their homes and possessions, kin and cattle.

It was the pathetic cries of the people that awakened the Ācārya more than nature's rebellion. What he saw was total chaos. Men, women, and children were trampling over one another in their bid for safety. Turning in the direction of the guru's cave, he found the pilgrims clambering over the hillside to reach high ground. The guru himself was not among them. The water had already begun to invade the tiny cave. With the safety of his guru in mind, he rushed thither and found the guru in the lotus posture, serene with eyes closed, his face an utter contrast to the anarchy outside. He realized that he was in no position to save himself and that it was his responsibility to rescue not only his teacher but also the woe-begone crowds on the hillside. Then, just as a massive tide was about to enter the cave, he repeated a mantra three times and placed his *kamaṇḍalu* near the opening. To the astonishment of everyone, the tide disappeared into the small water jar, and the fury of the flood at once began to diminish.

When Govindapāda returned to normal consciousness, people told him about the miracle. He seemed very pleased to hear about it, not so much because he had been saved—

which was immaterial—but because he remembered something that happened in the Himālayas in Sage Vyāsa's *āśrama* a long time ago. He said to the Ācārya: "Vyāsa was addressing the sages present on the immortality of Brahman. Everyone enjoyed the magnificent discourse, but I expressed a doubt. How was it possible for ordinary people to understand the terse aphorisms of the *Brahma-sūtra* without explanatory notes to accompany them? To this Vyāsa replied, 'Learned Govindapāda, it is true that, having written the simple epics and edited the Vedas, I wrote the involved epigrams of the *Brahmasūtra*. But don't worry. In due course, there will come to you as a disciple a very distinguished young ascetic who will do just what you have in mind. Please be patient until then. You will recognize this unique *sannyāsin* by his feat of controlling the Narmadā and ordering it into his *kamaṇḍalu*.' I know now that you are the boy Vyāsa spoke of. I have therefore this suggestion to make to you. Just as you contained the raging river in a small vessel, so do you compress the essence of all the Vedas into a commentary of the *Brahmasūtra*. As I told you, it is Vyāsa's own wish. Now, is there anything you wish to ask me?"

"O most distinguished Govindapāda, there is nothing that I desire except to remain forever immersed in Brahman bliss."

"Dear child, I am afraid that cannot be. Your mission on earth is to spread true knowledge among scholars as well as common folk. The former suffer from the delusion that logic can accomplish everything without reference to personal experience. The latter are a prey to superstition.

Your duty is to remove both kinds of ignorance and make them realize the primacy of the Self at the individual level. For their sake you will have to function in ordinary consciousness."

Govindapāda paused for a moment and added, "Today is the last day of my existence in this body. The wise of course are never deluded into thinking either that the body is permanent or that death is the end of life. It is just that I am casting off this frame which has served its purpose. You understand all this very well.

"Now listen to my last wish. Proceed to the holy city of Kāśī immediately and start instructing the people on how they can understand their real nature. Kāśī has many well-known scholars in all systems of philosophy. Hold discussions with them and guide them along the lines of right thinking. Though it does not take one far, logic is certainly useful in the initial stages of learning. Now I must go on my own journey, the journey into the Self. May the peace of *Brahman* be with you."

With this the venerable guru closed his eyes, raising his right hand in a gesture of benediction. An unearthly peace descended on him and radiated through his face. With a deep breath, he uttered that most awesome of syllables *Om* and remained silent. The arm gently dropped to the side.

6

ŚAṄKARA IS NOW ĀCĀRYA

In the days and weeks after I was accepted as a disciple by the Ācārya, many other disciples also came to him. In addition, the virtuous residents of Kāśī would flock to him to share in the knowledge of the Supreme Truth. They would also find, more often than not, that the Ācārya's instruction was so practical, so full of logical reasoning, and so scientific that they had to take nothing on faith.

The Ācārya would insist on all of us observing physical as well as mental discipline as an essential prerequisite to instruction in the *śāstras*. So one blazing noon in summer we found ourselves walking to the Gaṅgā to perform our midday rites. It was all right for the Ācārya who often transcended bodily consciousness, but we who were just beginners in yoga were roasting in the heat and tagged along marveling at his supernatural powers. We were glad to dive into the blue waters and didn't feel like getting out of there. But there were things to do, so we all started on our return trek to the camp.

The main thoroughfares of Kāśī were quite narrow as only the thoroughfares of a hoary, ancient city could be. The street we were walking on was no more than an alley, hardly a few feet wide. After we walked a little while, we found that our way was blocked by a dark, scruffy-looking person of a low caste with four dogs on leash and a stinking pot of toddy under his arm. We saw him approach from a distance but he showed no signs of slowing or moving aside to let us ass. According to custom, *cāṇḍālas* were required to step aside and make way for anyone going in the opposite direction. They were also required to maintain some distance as a mark of respect toward members of the higher castes. But this one apparently had no intention of observing that custom and kept coming at us.

The Ācārya, who always led the party, was a little upset about the impending encounter with the man, and worse, with his dogs. If he accidentally touched either, he would have to return to the river and take a purificatory bath. So he ordered the man to get out of the way. That would have normally knocked some sense into any outcaste and would have brought forth genuine apology, but this fellow posed a problem for the Ācārya instead.

He asked politely, "O greatest of the twice-born, when you ask me to step aside, do you suggest that matter should move away from matter or spirit from spirit? Is the sun, the jewel of the sky, reflected differently in the holy waters of the Gaṅgā than in my liquor pot? In terms of the all-pervading consciousness, is there any difference between a brahmin and an eater of dog flesh?

"You go about teaching, O Great Ācārya, that the only Reality is the non-dual *Brahman* which is immutable and unpollutable. Aren't you forgetting that the Spirit is beyond words and thought, unmanifest, beginningless, endless, and pure? How come you identify yourself and me with our bodies and not with the one shining Self? It's amazing how the greatest among us cannot escape duality, this feeling of difference, covered by the veil of *māyā!*"

The Ācārya then realized his error, which was the result of his social conditioning and upbringing but entirely contrary to his conviction. So he readily agreed with the *cāṇḍāla*.

"Indeed, you are right. The same blood flows in your veins and mine. The same Spirit resides in your body and mine. I was momentarily carried away by custom and I appreciate your pointing out my mistake. Many hear about the Truth of Vedanta and many meditate on the one *Ātman*, but few succeed in eradicating the sense of difference from their minds. Only he is my guru, be he a brahmin or *cāṇḍāla*, who is unshakably established in the conviction of the one Self behind the entire creation from the insect to Īśvara and in the belief that its apparent diversity is unreal. The Pure Consciousness throbbing in all of us as 'I' is the only Reality. Since you have exhibited this greatest understanding, you are my guru. Please accept my salutations."

While the Ācārya bowed his head to the *cāṇḍāla* in obeisance, it seemed to him that his interlocutor could be none other than Lord Śiva who came to teach him a lesson in practical Vedanta and remove the last vestige of duality from his mind. The four dogs could only be the four Vedas. It was his good fortune that he had this encounter with the Lord in the form of a lowly man who upheld the Vedantic ideal so firmly. He gratefully composed a hymn in praise of him.

"O Three-eyed Lord, when I look upon myself as a body, I am your servant. When I feel I am an individual *ātman*, I am part of you. And when I become aware of the Self, I am one with you. Such indeed is the eternal message of all scriptures to understand which yogis make endless efforts. Before that Supreme Truth, which is not different from my own Self, I bow my head."

The Ācārya was not imagining things. He did indeed see Śiva, the presiding deity of the city, and the dogs were the Vedas. The Lord was very pleased with the Ācārya's admission of his folly. He then blessed him and commanded him on his further mission.

"Since you have a real understanding of the Vedas and their purport, you should write a commentary on the *Brahmasūtra*, as already suggested by your guru, Govindapāda. After you have proved the superiority of *Advaita* to the satisfaction of all, establish several missions in different parts of the country, so that dharma will continue to be propagated and people will lead happy, contented lives."

The Ācārya was touched by the Lord's concern for him and His affection for him. He burst into spontaneous song. He was especially intrigued by the concept of Śiva and His consort being a single entity blessing the world. Either would be powerless without the other.

"I bow to the two auspicious deities, who are the essence of all learning, who wear the moon for their crest-jewel, and who have obtained each other through severe austerities. It is your eternal longing for each other that has resulted in your joint embodiment.

"There are thousands of other gods around who can confer mundane benefits on their devotees. But I am not interested in them or their gifts. All I want is to be able to worship your lotus feet forever. Whether one is a pupil or a master, *sannyāsin* or a householder, brahmin or untouchable, all one needs to do is surrender wholeheartedly to you to qualify for your grace.

"My mind is a monkey which ever roams the jungle of delusion, looking longingly at the bosoms of young maidens, and keeps leaping from one branch of desire to another. Please fill this mind of mine with a firm devotion to you.

"Devotion is that which attaches to its object like the *aṅkola* seed to the tree, iron filings to a magnet, the virtuous woman to her husband, and the river to the sea. Nothing else matters, for didn't the boorish hunter receive your grace who fanned your body with dirty sandals, washed it in his spittle, and fed it with leftover meat? But, when you tested him, he carved out his eye without the slightest hesitation and offered it to you.

"I know, Arch-Mendicant, that your food is poison, a serpent your ornament, and elephant hide your attire. So you have nothing to offer to other beggars like me. Why not then just grant me loyalty to your holy feet? That is enough for me for it replaces the darkest cloud of nescience in my heart with the enlightenment of *Brahman*.

> *ādyāvidyā hṛdgatā nirgatāsīt*
> *vidyā hṛdyā hṛdgatā tvatprasādāt.*

Unless they praise you, behold, worship, and meditate on you respectively, my tongue, eyes, hands, and mind are no use to me.

> *sā rasanā te nayane*
> *tāv eva karau, sa eva kṛtakṛtyaḥ*

yā ye yau yo bhargam
vadat īkṣate sadācaraḥ smarati.

"In truth, I cannot adequately describe your infinite greatness. You are regarded by Brahmā and Viṣṇu themselves as the Supreme Being. Other lesser gods are indeed like chaff in comparison with you."

7
SANANDANA EARNS THE NAME PADMAPĀDA

As commissioned by Lord Śiva and Vyāsa, the Ācārya wanted to start working on his commentaries, notably the one he planned on the *Brahmasūtra*. Kāśī was too crowded a place for any serious writing and the discourses were too time-consuming, so he decided to move up to Badarī in the Himālayas. For the next three years this was to be our home, and we were all glad that this was so for Badarī was a lovely place suspended on a hill slope right by the perennial Alakanandā. The surroundings were picturesque. We found here the time and the tranquillity needed for the Ācārya's monumental undertaking. And the king of the region agreed to take care of our needs down to the supply of writing materials.

Though engaged in the arduous task of writing most of the day, the Ācārya would still find time everyday to teach his disciples. These lessons were enjoyable and highly instructive. Any teacher, spiritual or secular, will be impressed by a student who is capable, and it cannot be helped if he is somewhat partial to him. Apparently, in my case it so happened that the Ācārya was pleased to notice that I was following his abstruse philosophical arguments three times as fast as my classmates. But my friends were not quite so pleased. They did not understand why I was being shown special attention by the teacher. The Ācārya was aware of their jealousy but chose not to say anything about it.

One day, as the other disciples were having a discussion with the Ācārya on the interpretation of a Vedic text, I happened to be away on the far side of the river running an errand. Then I suddenly heard my name being called from across the river and, looking up, I found the Ācārya was summoning me urgently. From the urgency in his tone, it seemed to me that there was some problem requiring my immediate attention. So I ran to the group as fast as I could to know the Ācārya's pleasure. Instead of answering me, the Ācārya simply kept smiling. The others merely stared at me as if I was a stranger. After a few minutes of this strange behavior on their part and puzzlement on mine, the Ācārya placed his hand on my shoulder and turned me around to face the river. The only thing I found was a neat row of white lotuses across the width of the river at two-foot intervals firmly standing up to the swift current. I turned back to the Ācārya with the same puzzled look as before, not knowing what the flowers had to do with me. The gracious Ācārya then explained what happened.

"Dear Sanandana, when I called out to you and asked you to come over at once, you took the shortest possible route to reach me. Without realizing what you were doing, you walked straight across the river and, as you took each step, a lotus sprang up to support your foot. You were not aware of it because your mind was entirely concentrated on reaching me right away as ordered. Normally, you would have crossed the river a hundred yards upstream where there is a rope bridge. Since your feet were supported by lotuses while crossing the river, you shall henceforth be known as Padmapāda."

This was news to me, but I soon realized that it was the Ācārya's own grace that enabled me to accomplish this feat which I knew I could not do on my own. It also occurred to me that the Ācārya might have wanted to show the other pupils that grace would flow where there was intense and unquestioning devotion. By now they were thoroughly ashamed of themselves and begged the Ācārya's forgiveness as well as mine. They would emulate my devotion to the teacher from now on. I never wanted to make my friends feel bad on my account. But it was the Ācārya's decision to magnify what little merit I had and there was nothing I could do about it.

8
THE ĀCĀRYA TESTED BY SAGE VYĀSA

The Ācārya composed many works and commentaries. In addition to brief treatises like *Upadeśa Sāhasrī* and *Ātma Bodha*, he commented on the *Bhagavadgītā*, the principal Upaniṣads, and of course the *Brahmasūtra*. They all supported the unified view of Truth as revealed in the Vedas.

With a view to making all these works available to scholars in the rest of the country, we began moving down south. We stopped first at a small, quiet town called Uttara Kāśī, on the northern bank of the Gaṅgā. We decided to spend a few days there because of its unusual scenic beauty. Our classes went on uninterrupted. One day, we had a particularly interesting session and a follow-up discussion. Just as we were about to finish, an old brahmin walked up to the Ācārya. With his flowing locks of auburn hair, innumerable bead necklaces, and bright shining eyes, he resembled the teacher of gods. He politely asked the Ācārya, "What are you discussing, O Learned *Sannyāsin*? And may I know who you are?"

We were somewhat annoyed by this interruption. We had had a rather long session and were about to disperse. This old man, who looked learned, had not heard of our great master whose name was known even to a child in a brahmin household. So I answered rather sharply, "Sir, this is the great Ācārya Śaṅkara, the well-known teacher of *advaita* and commentator on the *Brahmasūtra*. We were just discussing some of those aphorisms when we were interrupted."

The old man turned to me and smiled. "I am sorry I interrupted your lesson. I was passing by and heard a learned discussion going on. I was curious to know what it was. I am very pleased to meet the renowned Śaṅkara in person. Now, may I request the distinguished Ācārya here to expound any one of the *sūtras* for my benefit." He was still smiling, still polite.

The Ācārya was appropriately humble in the presence of the venerable visitor. "I bow to the feet of all writers of *sūtras.* I do not claim to be a master of *sūtra* literature. Yet if you ask me any question on the *Brahmasūtra*, I shall try my best to answer."

Then the brahmin quoted the first *sūtra* of the third chapter, *tadantarapratipattau raṁhati saṁpariṣvaktaḥ praśnanirūpaṇābhyām,* and waited.

The Ācārya began his exposition slowly and deliberately. "In its proper context, this statement means that when the soul is ready to inhabit a new body, it goes out sheathed in the subtle essence of the elements, but not the elements themselves. A discussion to this effect is found in the Upaniṣads."

The brahmin objected to this interpretation. "But one Upaniṣad says that the soul hangs on to the *gross* body like a leech and does not leave until it secures another gross body."

"No, Sir. What that text means is that the soul stretches itself out like a leech until it can find a suitable body along with all its psychomental impressions which are in turn dependent upon the past deeds of the old body. Missing the obvious truth, a number of schools of thought wrongly theorized on purely intellectual grounds. Some say that the senses go along with the soul to the new body. Others say it is accompanied by the mind. Still others believe that a soul jumps from one body to another like a monkey by itself. None of these is supported by the Vedas or the Upaniṣads."

The brahmin raised numerous other very valid objections which the Ācārya decisively met.

"It is said that the soul is enveloped by water at the time of its exit from the old body."

"No. 'Water' there implies the other two elements fire and air also. Water is specified just because of its preponderance in bodies in the shape of blood, semen, etc. Also, the scriptures say that the organs, too, accompany the soul, all of them of course in their subtle form."

A harmless inquiry thus turned into a learned controversy with attacks and counter-attacks and profuse references to the scriptures. Unlike in the other debates the Ācārya was used to, his opponent was as calm as he himself was and his fund of knowledge as inexhaustible. I was observing all this closely. My initial hostility to the stranger gave way to respect as he gave the Ācārya a hard time. Then I began to wonder whether the visitor might be the immortal Vyāsa who is said to reside in the Himālayas. I said so to the Ācārya.

The Ācārya confirmed my suspicion. He prayed to Vyāsa with folded hands. "O Immortal Sage, O Educator of Mankind, please forgive me my audacity in presuming to debate with you. All my learning I owe to you and your work. My disciples and I are honored by your visit. If you pardon my liberty, I beg you to review my commentary of your *Brahmasūtra* and correct it as necessary."

Vyāsa's graciousness was proverbial. "Śaṅkara, my child, I heard about you and your learning. I also heard that you wrote a commentary on my work, and wanted to see you in person. What I have seen just now and heard pleases me very much. I did intend to look at your commentary. This debate was only incidental."

Vyāsa then went over the commentary with undivided attention and superhuman rapidity. His heart brimming with joy, he addressed the Ācārya, "Dear Śaṅkara, I have thoroughly read your work. I cannot find any lapses in it to correct. I know that a student of Govindapāda's cannot make a mistake. The grammar is perfect. The methodology is effective. You first interpret the *sūtra* faithfully and within the framework of the scriptures, then discuss the opponent's point of view, and finally establish the definitive meaning. In all this, the powers of your reasoning are remarkable. What is most impressive however is the lucid style in which you discuss the profoundest concepts embodied in my *sūtras*. I bless you and your disciples. Not only that, in view of the great work you have ahead of you in controverting false doctrines, I am extending your life by sixteen years. I know you very much want to give up your body on the banks of the Gaṅgā in my presence, because your original mission of writing the commentaries has been fulfilled and you have completed your allotted life span. But you still have to establish a*dvaita* by refuting the practices of other sects that have been led astray for various reasons.

The Ācārya tried to protest saying that he had no desire to continue in the world but Vyāsa reminded him, "The purpose of this body and life is to help others in any manner possible. Right now, it is important that you enlighten the people of the land in the ways of the Spirit. Don't think that you will be living for yourself in the next sixteen years."

With bent head and downcast eyes the Ācārya indicated his submission to the sage's injunction. And Vyāsa left, pleased with the prospect of the people living their lives fruitfully and happily under the Ācārya's guidance.

The Ācārya also thought of his mother and his promise that he would be present when it was time for her to leave the world.

9
QUALIFICATIONS OF MASTER AND DISCIPLE

Ever since the Ācārya went to Kāśī for the first time, people wondered at his monumental learning and his ability for exposition. After all, when I met him at Kāśī, he was barely twelve years old, but he was already considered the best teacher in town. There was something about him that attracted people to him like a flower in bloom attracts the bees. Plus there was his philosophy which was so ennobling. He elevated every human being without exception to the level of the greatest god. And this was no special gift to any one individual, either. Human beings have always had the spark of divinity in them, once they realized it. Furthermore, every individual was bound to realize godhead, or better still, his selfhood, in due course even if one did nothing on one's own. But one could accelerate the process, provided one went about it in earnest. It was this respect for humanity, this boldness of statement that attracted everyone's attention. Prior to him prophets and saints and philosophers exhorted people on their conduct or suggested elaborate rituals or renunciation as a *sine qua non* for liberation. They also emphasized the sinful nature of humans, the need for an intermediary to present their case to God, the eternal distinction between God and humans, and so on.

All these approaches undoubtedly had their merit but were applicable only at lower levels of understanding. In the end one would not and should not be satisfied until one discovered one's roots in God and one's mystic identity with Him. The Ācārya proved this to be a distinct possibility here and now in his masterful logical formulations. He was of course merely interpreting the scriptures, those repertoires of human experience and direct revelation. Others were either afraid or incapable of this interpretation. No wonder the residents of Kāśī praised the boy Ācārya as Lord Viśvanātha Himself and declared that there never had been or would ever be one like him.

When he was teaching just his disciples after the public left, he was more a friend than a teacher handing down knowledge. He readily accepted suggestions from us. If they were untenable, he would indicate the problem with them. He would enliven the session with examples from real life, so great philosophic truths seemed very practical. We often wondered why we had not noticed a simple logical flaw or relation until it was pointed out to us.

I remember my first class session very well. The Ācārya and a few of us disciples sat in the dry sands of the Gaṅgā river bed one afternoon. The breeze was pleasant and the surroundings calm except for the swirl of the water. After a few minutes of silence, the Ācārya asked us to repeat this prayer after him:

saha nāv avatu
saha nau bhunaktu
saha vīryam karavāvahai
tejasvi nāv adhītamastu
mā vidviṣāvahai.

May the Lord protect us. May we enjoy our studies together. May we have the necessary strength for our studies. May the immortal sages be merciful toward us. May there be no ill-will among us. We always repeated this prayer every time we commenced a class session.

Then, before we began the study of the text, the Ācārya asked us, "My friends, do you know what qualifications a guru must have before he can undertake to teach any one?"

We said that we did not except that a guru should be someone like him.

"That's not the answer. A teacher must be capable of discussing the pros and cons of a problem. He must understand the pupil's questions and remember them for later occasions. He must have self-control, compassion, equanimity of temper, and a genuine desire to help his students. He should of course be a master of the scriptures. He must not have any attachments to objects seen or unseen. He must be a knower of Brahman and be established in it. He should never transgress any rules of conduct. He must be devoid of the shortcomings of ostentation, cunning, jealousy, falsehood, and egotism. His sole aim must be to impart knowledge to his pupils. Such are the characteristics of a worthy teacher."

Then out of curiosity I asked the Ācārya. "Revered Ācārya, it is our good fortune that we have such a guru. Are there any qualifications expected of the disciple, too?" The Ācārya said, "Indeed, there are, Padmapāda, and I am glad you asked. The disciple should first of all have a desire to learn. He must lead the life of a monk, having given up all his possessions and desire for anything worldly. He must have controlled his mind and senses, and be compassionate toward his fellow humans. He must approach the teacher in the proper manner. He should be able to grasp and retain the scriptures in his memory."

The Ācārya continued benignly. "Now that you and I know our respective roles, we may begin our study. Any study implies a subject studied. In our case, the proper subject is the knowledge of the Self because, if you know about the Self, you know about everything else."

He then slowly and systematically elaborated the notion of the Self. "There is no attainment superior to the knowledge of the Self. Any other knowledge is not knowledge in the real sense but ignorance. The results of actions are transitory; the knowledge of the Self leads to eternal Bliss. That Self is Existence. It is Consciousness. It is the only Reality. It is One. The many forms that we see are the projections of the mind and the senses and the intellect which are non-Self. They are therefore unreal. They function only as long as the Self shines through them. Their unreality can also be seen from the fact that they do not exist in dreamless sleep, while consciousness persists. The Self is the knower, the seer, the witness. Nothing else is needed to know it, just as we don't need a lamp to see another lamp. By turning away from the impressions of the senses in their gross form when awake and subtle form in dream, one gets an inkling of the nature of the Self.

"By repeated practice of the withdrawal of the senses and related disciplines, one is firmly established in the Self. One is free and is never born again. One is beyond sin and merit. The knower of the Self is without fear, because fear results from the recognition of an entity different from oneself. When there is but one Self and you are that, where is the fear?"

Then he gave us an example of how *Brahman* pervades the world. "The relationship between *Brahman* and the world is like that of the wood and a toy elephant made out of it. If you look at the wood as an elephant, then there is no wood. If you see the wood in the elephant, there is no elephant. Thus *Brahman* is the world, and the world disappears in *Brahman*."

He continued. "The realized person does not have any mind to speak of. Or one might say that his mind is like a crystal that reflects the color of whatever it comes in contact with. He is like the outward shape of a burnt rope, without any substance to it. He can get rid of his body at will. As long as he chooses to live in the body, he obeys the norms of the society, never does anything unacceptable to the society in which he happens to live. He lives solely for the benefit of others. His benevolent influence is always present whether he does anything or not. And he is under no obligation to do anything."

In just a few minutes and a few sentences, the Ācārya laid before us the essence of the Vedas. He added, "This is what we will be discussing over and over again in all our texts and commentaries. Do not expect to grasp all of it at once. It takes time for knowledge to dawn. It takes even more time for you to be able to live that knowledge and apply it to all that you do. For the time being, just meditate on what I have said today. In our next class and the following ones, you can ask all the questions that you want and raise all the doubts you feel like raising. And don't stop with questioning. Learn to *experience* the Self. Start from today. Start now."

It was getting time for our evening ablutions and prayers by then. Before we dispersed, we said the following benediction which also became a practice afterward.

May all people be happy. May the kings rule their lands in a just manner. May cows and brahmins be protected so that they can be of service to the community. May all the worlds be happy. May this land be free from disturbances. May we have timely rains that make the fields fertile. May the poor be well-provided, and the childless have children. May there be Peace!

10
KUMĀRILA IMMOLATES HIMSELF IN A SLOW FIRE

In our effort to popularize Vedanta through a systematic refutation of rival philosophies and quasi-philosophies, we traveled to Prayāga at the junction of the three rivers, Gaṅgā, Yamunā, and Sarasvatī. The last mentioned of these is said to be a subterranean stream, but the confluence of the other two is like the merging of the sky and the earth in eternal communion. The waters of the Gaṅgā at this point are a clear white, those of the Yamunā bluish. Poets have gone into raptures on the natural beauty of this expanse of water and the life in and around it. The faithful know that a bath at the Triveṇī, the trijunction, cleanses the murkiest of sins over a thousand past lives.

The Ācārya's intention in coming to Prayāga was to debate with Kumārila Bhaṭṭa, who was a ritualist and commentator on the *Mīmāṁsasūtra* of Jaimini. He not only wanted to vanquish him but also thought of having him write an explication of his own commentary on the *Brahmasūtra*. Kumārila was equally competent in both the dualistic and nondualistic branches of Vedanta. Besides, the Ācārya held him in high esteem as a man of impeccable character and integrity. But he was not prepared for what awaited him on his reaching Prayāga. As soon as he finished his ablutions at Triveṇī and made obeisances to the deity, news of Kumārila immolating himself in a slow fire reached him. It appeared that he did not have much time left. This was indeed tragic and the Ācārya and I rushed to where the great scholar was committing this violence against himself. It was a pathetic sight. There was a large heap of paddy husks in which he buried himself up to the neck.

The husks were about half burnt, and the smoke was thick and acrid. Enveloped in the smoke was the bright face of the brahmin shining like a red lotus at sunset. His eyes were closed serenely as if they were not part of the body that was being consumed by the fire extremely slowly. It looked as though the spirit had already transcended its physical limitations and was now merely a disinterested spectator of the gruesome process. His disciples stood by helplessly.

Though they had not met before, Kumārila instantly sensed the Ācārya's divine presence and gently opened his eyes. Welcoming him himself, he asked his disciples to receive him with honors appropriate for an ascetic of the highest order.

"O Great Kumārila," said the Ācārya, "I am indeed pained to see you in this condition. It is true that I had a desire to engage you in debate and claim victory over ritualism, but part of my intention, too, was to request you to write a commentary on my exegesis of the *Brahma-sūtra.* I now see that that is not going to be."

"Dear Śaṅkara, you are very kind. I have read your brilliant commentary and, if I had not vowed to immolate myself, I would gladly have written an explication of it. Of course, it would take eight thousand verses to do justice to the single concept of superimposition which, as you have shown, provides a clue to our mistaking the object for the subject. But no matter. All that is irrelevant now. However I consider it my good fortune to have seen your holy form just before my bodily extinction."

Deeply touched, the Ācārya replied. "If you permit me, O learned one, I can save you from the impending end by sprinkling a few drops of consecrated water from my *kamaṇḍalu*. I am sure I will have divine support in my effort, seeing it is a worthy cause. Please allow me to save you and restore your body."

Smiling wanly, Kumārila answered, "I know you are capable of such a feat, and more. It would be child's play for you who in a trice controlled the raging Narmadā. But I cannot accept your offer for that would make me a coward and a liar. You should not ask me to set a bad example by retracting my vow which I undertook for a specific reason."

Then in order to explain to the Ācārya and the others the reason for his present action, he narrated the events in his early life before he came to be known as a great scholar. "I have committed two sins which call for purification through fire. One is that in my commentaries on Jaimini's *sūtras*, I have rejected the idea of God, placing the Vedas above Him. Of course my point has been that since the Veda is self-sufficient, there is no need for positing an external God to prove its validity or have Him as the efficient cause of the world. I have however never denied the Self or *Brahman*, for that would be denying my own existence and the existence of the creation including the Vedas.

"Denial of a benevolent Lord for whatever reason is unpardonable. The other sin is more unpardonable. As you know, the Buddhists who are opposed to the Vedas, have a stranglehold on the people in some parts of the country. In order to point out their erroneous reasoning and untenable conclusions, I debated with as many of them as I could in my younger days. But, not knowing their particular system of dialectics, I had no ready answers to their counter-questions sometimes. So I thought the best way would be to study with one of their own teachers under the guise of a Buddhist monk. I successfully did this for some time, but my identity was betrayed when I inadvertently shed tears when one of them abused the Vedas. They found out that I was a brahmin who infiltrated their camp to know their secrets. As a punishment these champions of nonviolence decided to do away with me. Finding that I had overstayed my welcome at the monastery, I quietly left.

"In course of time, I reached the court of King Sudhanvan of Ujjain who received me with great courtesy and humility. I noticed however that he was surrounded by Buddhist monks. I wanted to rescue the king from their deceptive teachings. So, as if addressing a cuckoo bird in the tree outside the court, I said, 'O cuckoo, your voice is very sweet, but it would be sweeter and more delightful to my ears if you were not mixed up with all those ugly crows around you.'

"My words had the desired effect. The monks turned red with anger and were hissing like trampled snakes. They promptly challenged me to a debate but this time I had no problem dealing with them. They were soon put in their place.

"At this juncture, King Sudhanvan intervened to say that, since mere book learning and logic were no proof of the superiority of one philosophy over another, he would hold a test. The Buddhists and I agreed to this proposal. Though I did not have the slightest doubt about the potency of the Vedas, I thought this would be a good opportunity for me to show once and for all that the Buddhist arguments were spurious. The king announced that he would accept the religion of whichever party could jump off the high cliff outside the city unhurt as the superior one. The Buddhists who thought argumentation was all there was to religion were aghast and could not take up the challenge I went up the hill and after a brief prayer told myself, 'If the Vedas are eternally true, no harm shall befall me.'

"With the thought of the Supreme Being in my mind, I closed my eyes and jumped down unharmed. As I came down lightly as a ball of cotton, the spectators cheered me loudly and observed that it was no wonder that the Vedas protected one who put one's total faith in them. But because I questioned for a brief moment what was unquestionable and by implication doubted what was beyond doubt when I said '*If* the Vedas are eternally true,' I lost one of my eyes.

"The king now began to doubt the efficacy of the religion of the monks. The people came from all over the city to pay their respects to me as a performer of great miracles. The Buddhists however argued that this was still no proof of the superiority of the Vedic religion as the feat could easily be performed by an ordinary magician or by one who had mastered certain mantras or taken certain drugs. The king then said, 'All right, I shall now give you another test which will be final. The party that fails the test will be driven away from the kingdom and I shall proclaim the winner's religion as the religion of the land.' He briefly consulted his ministers and had a sealed earthen pot brought in. We were asked to identify the contents of the pot. The Buddhists and I asked for a day's time and retired for the night. The monks meditated on the problem and I prayed to the Vedic god Āditya for enlightenment. He appeared in a vision and gave me the answer. The following day the assembly hall was overflowing with spectators as we entered and took our seats. The king first asked the monks whether they knew what was inside the pot. The readily replied that there was a snake. He next turned to me, and I said that inside the pot was Viṣṇu resting on the coils of the great serpent Ādiśeṣa. On hearing this the king was somewhat taken aback, because he knew that he had an ordinary snake put in the pot. At that moment a divine voice was heard above, 'O Glorious King, what the brahmin says is true.' Upon opening the pot the king found to his surprise Viṣṇu on Ādiśeṣa. His faith in the Vedas had now increased a thousandfold. The Buddhists were banished from the kingdom.

"But, O Great Ācārya, all that is history. I am immolating myself now. Of course your very sight renders the great sinner sinless and this rite is perhaps meaningless. If I had met you earlier I would not have undertaken this punishment of myself.

"Now may I make a suggestion to you and seek a favor from you. The suggestion is that you should go to the city of Māhiṣmatī and debate with my disciple, Maṇḍana Miśra. Defeating him is tantamount to defeating the entire group of ritualists, since he is superior even to me in his mastery of Vedic philosophy. Then you can ask him to write the commentary on your work. The favor I seek is that you initiate me into *sannyāsa* and impart the knowledge of Brahman to me." The compassionate Ācārya then taught Kumārila the absolute non-difference between the individual and Brahman and the relationship of the individual to the phenomenal world. He stayed there for some more time in silent meditation praying for the great Bhaṭṭa who presently merged in universal consciousness.

11
BHĀRATĪ WEDS VIŚVARŪPA

In a small village by the river Śoṇa, there lived a brahmin whose only child Bhāratī was the cynosure of all eyes. She mastered all the *śāstras* under the guidance of her father. News of her good looks and great learning spread as far south as Māhiṣmatī on the Narmadā where Viśvarūpa had just returned from his studies with a great reputation as a *mīmāṁsā* scholar. Enthusiastic reports of Viśvarūpa's learning and immense wealth also reached Bhāratī. They both knew instantly that they were destined for each other but were too embarrassed to broach the subject before their parents. They began to pine for each other.

Viśvarūpa's father Himamitra was the first to notice a peculiar change in his son. "What's the matter, son? You don't seem to be your normal self. You don't spend much time any more in the performance of rituals or the recitation of the Veda. If something is bothering you, you can freely confide in me. They say that a father is like a friend to his grown-up son. Your mother is also worried about you and suggested that I ascertain from you the reason for your indisposition. Tell me, my boy, what is it?"

"Your son thanks you for your solicitude. Ever since I was born I have received nothing but tender love and affection from you and mother. I should have no worry on that account at all. We do not lack possessions. I have yet to come across a scholar who can defeat me in dialectics. I have never strayed from the path of virtue. However I do have something on my mind and, with your permission, I shall speak up, though it is embarrassing for me.

"Tradition says that a man who enters the second stage of life must look for a suitable wife in order to acquire eligibility for the performance of certain rituals. I feel I ought to find for myself a partner in life to carry on the dharma of our community. In this regard I must tell you that I have heard of an exquisitely graceful, learned, and virtuous young woman who is the daughter of Viṣṇumitra of Śoṇapura. Pray contact this good brahmin and see if he considers me a suitable husband for his beloved daughter. Please forgive me if I have been too bold in my reply to you."

With a knowing smile on his face, Himamitra went inside to consult with his wife. He then dispatched two emissaries to Śoṇapura to negotiate an alliance with Viṣṇumitra. The white-robed, staff-carrying, travel-worn messengers briefly gave their message to Viṣṇumitra. "Our master, Himamitra, sends his greetings to you and asks that you offer your daughter Bhāratī's hand in marriage to his son Viśvarūpa. We have considered all factors, and we believe that they make an excellent couple. We await your word on this proposal."

"Gentlemen, I am very pleased to hear your proposal. Ordinarily, it is the bride's parents who are expected to initiate these proceedings but you have spared me that trouble. Please make yourselves comfortable and refresh yourselves, while I discuss the matter with my wife. I might tell you right away that I am agreeable to the proposal, but after all a mother knows her daughter's mind better." So saying Viṣṇumitra went looking for his wife.

The lady, somewhat suspicious by nature and at any rate wary about her daughter's future, was not too sure. "These people are from a far-off land. We know nothing about the groom or his parents or their property. I want my daughter to lead a happy life forever. You know that according to the *śāstras* we have to consider the seven-fold qualification of family tradition, character, age, looks, learning, wealth, and upbringing of the groom. In this case, what information do we have?"

"I know, dear, that it is customary in the world for the bride to be attracted by the groom's appearance, her mother by his wealth, and her father by his learning. So I don't blame you for being concerned about your daughter's married life. While it is true that we do not know a great deal about these people, I do know that Viśvarūpa is a distinguished disciple of Kumārila Bhaṭṭa. He has already vanquished many prominent Buddhist and Jaina scholars and helped establish the superiority of Vedic ritual. And that's more important to me than material possessions. Learning is impervious to the vicissitudes of fortune. Money and property are constantly coveted by relatives, neighbors, and rulers, but one who is learned is respected by one and all. So I cast my vote in favor of Viśvarūpa. It is not proper that we keep our daughter too long in our home now that she is at the right age for matrimony."

Viṣṇumitra's wife had to yield albeit reluctantly. She yet wanted to have the last word on the subject. "Enough of your arguments. Let's try to know Bhāratī's mind. If she is agreeable, I am agreeable." She was still hoping that Bhāratī might raise some objections to the proposed alliance or make some stipulations to ensure that the groom was indeed what all he was represented to be.

Though modest by nature, Bhāratī could not conceal her

joy upon hearing the proposal. Thanking her favorite deity, she readily consented to marry Viśvarūpa. Moreover, using her proficiency in astrology, she set a date for the wedding ceremony some two weeks from then.

The intense feeling of joy was also shared by Viśvarūpa when he heard about Bhāratī's decision. His dreams really came true. No more pining or sleeplessness. On the appointed day he started for the bride's place accompanied by his parents. His face beamed with pride. His mind rejoiced at the thought of uniting with Bhāratī. He justified his eagerness by recalling how Śiva, the killer of Kāma and the controller of animal passion, Himself could not wait to wed Himavān's daughter. He was only an ordinary mortal smitten with love for the divinely charming Bhāratī.

As the groom arrived in full wedding regalia on the banks of the Śoṇa, there was great jubilation among the guests and relatives in both parties. An interminable exchange of jokes and pleasantries began. Everyone teased everyone else of the slightest acquaintance at the least provocation. Himamitra and Viṣṇumitra congratulated themselves on their great good fortune. Soon, under skies lit up with fireworks, amid the blaring of musical instruments and pounding of the drums and the shouting of Vedic mantras, Bhāratī and Viśvarūpa were joined in holy matrimony. The bride and groom vainly tried to maintain their composure, but their faces betrayed their surging happiness as they went round the sacrificial fire three times to cement their relationship for eternity. Just to become friends, it is said, seven steps together would do. Unspoken promises of love for each other sprouting from the depths of their souls were witnessed by the crackling fire. To the scholars among the guests they appeared to suit each other as perfectly as a word and its connotation.

Laden with rich presents the relatives and friends slowly left. After a few days it was time for the newlyweds themselves to depart. This is ever a crucial moment for the bride's parents because it is the bride who leaves the parents' home to spend the rest of her life with her husband. Bhāratī's parents addressed their son-in-law, the newest member of their family, in a voice choked with emotion

"We now trust to your care this little child with heavy hearts. She is used to having her way in work and play, and is very sensitive to criticism. We have had no occasion to train her in household duties, so you may find her somewhat deficient in that regard. Please ask your mother to bear with her and treat her like her own daughter. You must take good care of her and coach her lovingly in the art of being a housewife. Be a brother to her and forgive her omissions. Be a friend to her and guide her in all her actions. You will find her a gentle and lovable soul."

Turning to their daughter, they added, "Bhāratī, dear, the time has come for you to leave us and head for your husband's home. If you conduct yourself well over there, it redounds to your credit as well as ours. It's hard for you and us to realize that you are no longer a child and that you have entered a new stage of life. Please remember that not everybody is as forgiving as one's parents. You have a different and very onerous role to play now.

There are a few rules of conduct enjoined upon all wives in our tradition and it is proper that you observe them. Do not eat before your husband has eaten. Do not wear ornaments or flowers when he is away. When he is angry, you be calm. Do not directly look at strangers when you talk to them even in your husband's presence, lest he should think that you do the same in his absence. When your husband returns home from work, offer him cool water and refreshments. For a faithful wife there is nothing as satisfying as ministering to her husband's needs. Do not waste time in idle gossip with the neighbors. Consider your husband's parents as your own and his brothers as your own."

Viṣṇumitra then clasped his daughter to his bosom and with tearful eyes whispered in her ear, "My child, please forgive me and your mother for saying these things to you. You know all the customs and obligations yourself. We are very proud of you. You know that these commandments are not meant to insult the bride but to ensure domestic harmony at her husband's place. As a matter of fact, a good husband is in every way as devoted to his wife as she is to him. These do's and don'ts only suggest adjustments needed for the housewife's role in the family. No inferiority of the wife is implied. There are households where the woman is regarded with greater respect than the man. I hope you understand."

Bhāratī tried to smile bravely as she said, "I understand, father." When she bent down to bow to his feet in formal leave-taking, warm tears rolled down her bejewelled nose and drenched his toes. One could have hardly suspected that this bashful new wife was the accomplished scholar who would later monitor the celebrated debate between her husband and the great Ācārya.

12
ENCOUNTER WITH MAṆḌANA MIŚRA

Along with the news of Viśvarūpa's marriage, his fame as a scholar also spread far and wide. In fact, he was considered such a formidable scholar and respected so highly in his part of the country that people hesitated to refer to him by name. They just called him Maṇḍana Miśra, the jewel among the scholars. Simultaneously, Bhāratī's attainments also came to be known in her father-in-law's home. Because she had been accepted as a lady of great learning both at her father's and her father-in-law's places, she was given the nickname of Ubhaya Bhāratī.

Now, as suggested by the dying Kumārila, the Ācārya traveled toward Māhiṣmatī with a view to converting Maṇḍana to Vedāntism. It took almost a month for us to walk from Prayāga to the Narmadā. The city was situated on the northern bank. The Ācārya completed his morning rites and rested a while in the cool breeze coming from the river. Just before midday we went into town and asked for directions to Maṇḍana's house of some women who were drawing water from a well. They knew the house right away and told us to go to the largest building in the center of the town. As a further means of identification, they said that that by the wide gates of the house there would be many parrots repeating philosophical discussions among themselves: "Are the Vedas self-validated? Is action better than contemplation? Is the world real or apparent?"

We were amazed at this piece of information. Wondering about the greatness of Maṇḍana, we arrived at the large mansion with a cluster of small houses and assembly halls around it. The vast gardens and the structures looked magnificent in the bright sun. They all loudly proclaimed the owner's affluence and his diligence in their maintenance.

As we got ready to enter the compound, we found that the gate was locked. The Ācārya told us to wait beneath the trees and went to the back of the house. Thanks to a tall *neem* tree by the wall, the sixteen-year-old Ācārya had no difficulty landing on the other side just where Maṇḍana was performing a *śrāddha* ceremony in honor of his dead ancestors. By the power of his *tapas*, Maṇḍana was able to invoke the presence of Vyāsa and Jaimini, whose feet he was washing as a prelude to the ceremony. The two sages recognized the Ācārya and smiled, and the Ācārya bowed to them in humility. But Maṇḍana was completely taken by surprise at the arrival of a boy *sannyāsin* during the performance of a sacred ceremony.

It was inauspicious to see a *sannyāsin* on such an occasion, which was why he had the front entrance locked. And this *sannyāsin's* mode of entry was most unorthodox. He was very upset by the rude interruption and demanded to know whence the boy came. "*Kuto muṇḍī*?" "Where are you from?" which question, if interpreted differently, could mean "To what extent are your shaven?"

The Ācārya knew he was in control of the situation. He chose to descend upon Maṇḍana, literally. He was going to demand a debate. It was certain, on the basis of past experience, that the ritualistic philosophy had not a leg to stand on. So the Ācārya was sparring with him, deliberately provoking him as much as possible. Though he had much regard for Maṇḍana, he yet decided to indulge in a little levity with the older scholar.

"As you see, I am shaven from the throat upwards."

"I don't mean that," explained Maṇḍana. "I am asking you about the path you follow, the order to which you belong, *panthās te pṛcchyate mayā*."

Taking advantage once again of the ambiguity in Maṇḍana's sentence construction the Ācārya queried, "Oh, you talked to the path? What did it say?"

Maṇḍana realized that it was hard for him to obtain a straight answer from the boy. "It said that you are the son of a widow."

"It said that *you* are the son of a widow? Then it must be true. I am very sorry to hear that." The more Maṇḍana was exasperated, the more the Ācārya enjoyed the situation.

"Boy, are you drunk? *Pītā kimu surā?*"

Seizing upon the adjectival meaning of *pīta,* the Ācārya hurled the question back. "So you want to know if toddy is yellow? No, I am afraid it's white."

"Ah, I see you know well the color of toddy," insinuated Maṇḍana.

"But you know its taste."

Maṇḍana, now quite worked up, asked, "Is your incoherent chatter due to eating rotten meat? *Matto jātaḥ kalañjāsī?*" Again deliberately misconstruing the question to mean "You who are born of me, have you eaten rotten meat?" the Ācārya said, "Like father, like son."

Maṇḍana decided to attack the Ācārya on another front.

"Say, I am curious about something. You have abandoned the sacred thread and the auspicious tuft of hair on the back of your head, maybe because they are too heavy. Yet I see you carry a donkey's load of rags on your shoulder." This was a reference to the requirements of the order of *sannyāsa* as opposed to those of a householder.

"True, but that is still better than carrying the burden of a wife, as your father had done. And look at the result," the Ācārya said pointing to Maṇḍana. "You don't seem to understand this simple truth. No wonder you understand little of *Brahmavidyā*."

"O yes, I know all about it. *Sannyāsa* is going about in rags with a bunch of loafers begging food as you don't have to work for it. It's a grand excuse for vagrancy."

"Is that right? Then what about the householder? Because he can't remain celibate and control his sensuality, he lives with a woman as a slave of his lust."

"How can you vilify women? A woman conceived you and raised you. This is gross ingratitude."

"Then may I ask how come you want to sleep with a woman like an animal, knowing that you originated from her womb and nursed at her breast?"

Opening another line of argument, Maṇḍana commented, "Neglecting the sacred fires enjoined in the scriptures is tantamount to filicide."

"Neglecting the study of one's own self as identical with *Brahman* is suicide."

"You are a thief. You entered my house by stealth."

"You are the real thief. You have not been feeding *sannyāsins* as required by the *śāstras*. You are depriving them of their share of food."

At his wit's end, Maṇḍana muttered aloud. "I shouldn't be wasting my time and holding up my ceremony talking to a boor like you. Anyway, where are real *sannyāsins* and sages in this dark age? People like you are parasites on the society."

"Where are the sacred fires in this dark age? Where are the people who have attained the pleasures of heaven through rituals? Men like you camouflage their real intention of enjoying the company of women when they pretend to perform them."

Insults and counter-insults were thus exchanged by the two great personages, but there was a difference in tone. The senior man Maṇḍana was proud and indignant, the Ācārya was merely content with a witty rejoinder to each of his attacks. The Ācārya was thoroughly enjoying himself.

At this point the venerable Vyāsa intervened and chided Maṇḍana for his discourtesy to the visiting *sannyāsin.* Regardless of everything, any visitor at meal time must be treated as Viṣṇu Himself and honored. Maṇḍana then graciously invited the Ācārya to have food with him upon which the latter said, "I have not come here for food, Learned Maṇḍana. The alms that I beg of you are those of a debate. My only interest in life is to spread Vedānta as the ultimate knowledge to all corners of the earth. One who ignores Vedānta lives a mere life of rituals and sacrifices both of which in themselves are meaningless. They cannot rescue you from the *saṁsāric* cycle. If you accept the supremacy of Vedānta, then there is no need for a debate. If you don't, let's debate and stipulate that the vanquished shall join the order of the victor."

"Agreed. We will certainly have a debate. Even the thousand-tongued Ādiśeṣa cannot withstand me in public debate. So I am not worried about you. I shall then have a chance to expose some of the audacity of your teachings. I always look forward to meeting competent opponents in argument, and thus your arrival is most welcome. You and your disciples may remain as my guests for the duration of the proceedings. We shall start the debate tomorrow."

One of the formalities for a debate of this sort was that there should be a moderator to observe the discussion and declare the winner at the end. So Maṇḍana requested the two sages to act jointly as moderators, but they politely declined suggesting that the honor should go to his wife, Bhāratī. The Ācārya had no objection to it.

The Ācārya then joined us at the front entrance where we were all waiting eagerly. He regaled us with the details of his interesting visit with Maṇḍana and informed us about the debate scheduled for the next day.

13
THE GREAT DEBATE

As stipulated, the next morning the Ācārya was ready for the debate with Maṇḍana. The morning was pleasant. There was a gentle breeze from the river. The sun was out in his full splendor, as if dressed up to attend the debate. Already scores of citizens had arrived and occupied vantage points. Some merely chose comfortable places in the hall such as corners or pillars to lean against when they got tired. The disciples of Maṇḍana and we sat facing one another behind the raised platforms meant for our respective gurus. Presently Maṇḍana and Bhāratī entered the hall, acknowledging the greetings of all assembled, including those of the Ācārya.

Bhāratī, as previously arranged, presided over the proceeding. She made her opening remarks. "Welcome to the scholars and residents of Māhiṣmatiī. Welcome to the great *sannyāsin,* Paramahaṁsa Ācārya Śaṅkara, who wishes to debate with my husband, Viśvarūpa, whom you have all honored with the title, Maṇḍana Miśra. It has been agreed to by both contestants that I act as the moderator and name the winner at the end. But since I have to attend to a number of household duties and make arrangements for food, I will not be able to watch the debate all the time. So I shall give each contestant a garland, and the contestant whose garland remains fresh at the end of the debate shall be declared the winner. The debate shall now commence." She handed out the garlands she had brought for the purpose.

The debate started with a statement of their theses by the two debaters. Maṇḍana spoke first. "I accept the authority of the Vedas. Their main teaching is that merit can be acquired through the performance of rituals in the prescribed manner. One who performs these rituals will go to heaven and there dwell in the company of Indra and the celestial damsels. When the merit is exhausted, he will return to earth so that he can acquire more merit for a longer stay in the world of gods. The Vedas also contain related commandments the observance of which is a prerequisite for the performance of the rites." The audience applauded this very clear opening statement from Maṇḍana.

Then it was the Ācārya's turn. He began in his deep, rich voice that resonated in the hall. "I also accept the authority of the Vedas. Their main purport for me however is this: *Brahman* alone is real; the phenomenal world is an illusion; and the individual soul is identical with *Brahman*. The parts of the Veda containing descriptions and injunctions pertaining to ritual are subordinate to the major part that deals with the knowledge of the Self and the ways of its acquisition. Rituals can only lead to karma both good and bad, and either kind prevents one from realizing one's Self." There was a longer applause.

Tension mounted in the hall as both parties followed up their theses with volleys of searching questions and suitable responses. It was interesting to note that the same scriptures could be viewed from two different perspectives both equally plausible and equally convincing.

Maṇḍana challenged the Ācārya. "Learned Ascetic, you firmly believe that the individual soul and *Brahman* are identical. What proof do you have of this in the scriptures?"

"There are categorical statements like *tat tvam asi*, THAT you are; *tad aham ātmānam eva vedāham brahmāsmīti*, therefore know that you are Brahman; *tasmāt sarvam abhavat,* all this was born of that, etc., etc."

"But those statements carry no special meaning. They are rather like the endings of the formulas used in rituals, such as *svāhā, vaṣaṭ, phaṭ*, etc."

"But the statements that I have quoted *do* have meaning in the language unlike the magic syllables you mention. So they cannot be equated."

"Let's say that they are meaningful. Even so, they are merely statements extolling the greatness of the sacrifice. There are no other statements referring to an ever-existing *Brahman* to be realized. Sometimes they merely serve as injunctions pertaining to rituals. They are of no greater significance than that."

"Not so. These passages occur in the context of the exposition of the Self, and not while discussing the merits of sacrifice. As regards the existence of *Brahman*, there are unambiguous texts attesting to that, e.g. '*Ātman* alone existed at first,' 'The Real alone was there in the beginning,' '*Brahman* is immutable,' etc."

"Perhaps they are then intended for meditation. When you meditate that you are Brahman, the potency of the sacrifice increases. Beyond that, they do not signify much."

"But, Learned Maṇḍana, you know that all instructions regarding meditation in the Vedas are put in the imperative, 'Meditate on the mind as *Brahman*,' 'Meditate on the organs of sense as *Brahman*,' etc., but *tat tvam asi* is a statement, an assertion."

"Mere descriptions or statements would be without purpose unless they exhort people to meritorious actions. These statements therefore mean that if you meditate on yourself as *Brahman* then you will be liberated. So, too, in the case of all other non-dual descriptions in the scripture. They are all designed to help the seeker attain liberation."

"What you have just said makes liberation an *effect* of a certain action. Anything that is an effect of something else is impermanent and therefore not of the nature of Reality. Meditations, rituals, etc. are actions with a promised or desired result. *Brahman*, on the other hand, is knowledge. And it is knowledge or awareness that is the real goal of *mokṣa*. *Mokṣa* is not something you enjoy, as you would enjoy food, sex, or kingship, but just being your real self beyond body, beyond mind, beyond sleep. This is not a new condition or effect but is something natural."

Maṇḍana felt that it was necessary to yield a little. "Suppose we say that 'You are *like Brahman*' rather than 'You *are Brahman*.' Then it would be easy to comprehend the source of creation as Intelligence. One knows this by comparing this source with oneself who is intelligent."

"There are problems with that approach. What does the similarity consist of? Omniscience? Omnipotence? Eternality?"

"A man's soul is similar to *Brahman* in that both are eternally conscious. But in respect of all-pervasiveness, there is some difference because the individual soul is enveloped by nescience, whereas *Brahman* is Pure Knowledge."

"I don't see why you want to hang on to any difference while accepting that both *Brahman* and *Ātman* are eternally intelligent. Why not get rid of your fear and say that they are one as stated a thousand times in the Veda?"

Maṇḍana now suggested a more direct proof for the difference between the individual soul and *Brahman*. "In our experience, we don't feel that our souls are the same as *Brahman*, the Supreme Intelligence. How can something that is intuitively invalid be accepted as the Truth?"

"What you call intuition is a trick of the mind whose nature is ignorance. There is another problem. In order to negate something, it must have an existence of its own that is perceptible or known to have been experienced. In this case, we haven't *seen* the Ātman, so neither negations nor difference can be predicated of it."

Maṇḍana still could not bring himself to accept the supreme unity of the individual and universal souls.

"Suppose that we don't talk about perception or intuition to understand the relation between humans and their Creator. We know that the Creator is all-knowing whereas humans are ignorant. How can a clay pot be identical with the potter?"

"Your illustration is inappropriate because one can compare only two sentient or two insentient objects, and not one sentient and one insentient one."

"No, my example is satisfactory because I hold the Creator and the creature, the potter and the pot, are distinct. Self-knowledge cannot eliminate these differences."

"What you are saying is true only if you are talking about the knowledge of the physical self and not the ineffable Self, the Great Intelligence."

"I still maintain that *Brahman* is a distinctive entity and acquisition of knowledge about it will not equate the individual with it."

"What kind of *Brahman* are you talking about? Someone with attributes like Rāma, Kṛṣṇa, or Indra or the one Attributeless, Indivisible, and Absolute Reality? In the case of the former the differences do persist. In the case of the latter, the question of distinction does not arise. When the entire creation is suffused with that spirit, where is the separateness?"

"The Vedic passage that says that the individual and the Creator live in the cavity of one's heart establishes the difference, doesn't it?"

"That dualistic passage, along with others of similar import, refers to the relative and not the absolute existence. But what the non-dualistic texts do is to present the sort of knowledge that is unique. They are a revelation. They are unaffected by any other passage. They are self-existing and self-validating."

Since the learned Maṇḍana also accepted the incontrovertible authority of the Vedas, he had no further arguments to offer. However the discussion continued for many days and covered a variety of related topics. The two debaters matched wits and often changed their offense and defense strategies. In spite of his initial hostility to the Ācārya, as the debate progressed, Maṇḍana's regard for him grew. And the Ācārya was quite impressed with the range and depth of knowledge of this great disciple of Kumārila. But Kumārila Bhaṭṭa himself surrendered before the Ācārya's superior logic and aptness of quotation as demonstrated in his writings and accepted instruction from him. Maṇḍana, once he found out the shortcomings of his philosophy, gladly followed suit.

14
MAṆḌANA'S DEFEAT AND CONVERSION

On the eighteenth day of the great debate, in the presence of all assembled scholars and spectators, Bhāratī announced her decision in a clear voice. "From the fresh garland around the Ācārya's neck and from my own observation, I am of the firm opinion that the Ācārya is the winner. My husband's arguments, scholarly though they were, could not stand up to the Ācārya's superior logic. It was not merely a question of logic, either. There is something final and authoritative about the Ācārya's propositions that compel me to declare him the winner in this debate. I would have, naturally, liked the result to be otherwise, but I must be impartial. I bow to the Ācārya's great erudition and unparalleled forensic ability."

She continued. "However, the Ācārya's victory is not complete. He must defeat me, Maṇḍana's consort in life and learning. Until then my husband cannot be asked to renounce his family and possessions." Turning to the Ācārya she added, "You may indeed be the master of all knowledge, since you have already gotten the better of my renowned husband. I should nevertheless debate with you myself."

The Ācārya was somewhat surprised to hear this. He respected the lady for her scholarship and had no qualms about her being the umpire for the debate. But entering into a debate with her was quite another matter.

"Distinguished wife of Maṇḍana Miśra, I am well aware of your great reputation for scholarship. I know you will be every bit as worthy an opponent as your husband in debate. But I am afraid I cannot enter into any contest with a woman."

Bhāratī knew of this irrational tradition. "What difference does it make when your doctrines are under attack? Is it not your duty to uphold them? We have several examples from history: the venerable Yājñavalkya discoursed with Gārgī; Janaka engaged Sulabhā in a lengthy argument. Those sages had no objection to a contest with a woman. I don't understand why you are hesitant."

The Ācārya saw Bhāratī's point and agreed to the debate. This round of arguments was even more delightful to watch. Bhāratī, who had observed the Ācārya's technique in discussion, tried to forestall many of his criticisms of ritualism, and the Ācārya had to come up with new objections. This revised strategy however did not take her too far, for the Ācārya's inventiveness was unlimited and his memory prodigious. Even though she was no less resourceful herself, in the end, she had to admit that he was invincible in the exposition of all conventional knowledge. So she decided to test him in *Kāma Śāstra*, the science of sexual love, a subject that was quite respectable and one with which he, as a *sannyāsin*, was unlikely to have any acquaintance. This might be her only chance to save herself and her husband from certain defeat.

She addressed the Ācārya, "I grant you that in the discussions we have had so far, you have the upper hand. You have answered all my questions and refuted my arguments. Yet I can't admit that you are a master of all learning until you have shown that you have a good grounding in sex education, too. You know that it is one of the sixty-four traditional branches of learning. Now, tell me, what are the various forms and expressions of love? What is the nature of sexual love and what are its physical loci? What is the effect of the waxing and waning moons on sex urge in men and women? How can a man gain the company of a woman who is recalcitrant and *vice versa*?"

The Ācārya hesitated to answer these questions. It was not as though he could not answer them for he had studied Vātsyāyana along with other classics. But then his theoretical knowledge might not be enough to come up with the best answers. He was also worried about the propriety of a *sannyāsin* answering such questions. In view of these considerations, he simply said to Bhāratī, "Learned Bhāratī Devī, I know you have every right to question me on *Kāma Śāstra*, but as an ascetic I am not expected to know much about it. However, given a month's time, I shall acquire the requisite knowledge on the topic and will answer all your questions. You know that it is customary among debaters to ask for and be given sufficient notice before discussions. I didn't need any for the other subjects, but in this case I do, for obvious reasons." Bhāratī knew that at least for the time being she had him in a spot and readily granted him the requested extension of time.

* * * * * * *

Our party left Maṇḍana's place forthwith and moved to the forest outside Māhiṣmatī. We were all wondering how we could help the Ācārya in his bid to win the debate with Bhāratī, but could not come up with any practical plan. Then, just ahead of us, we saw a number of dignitaries and court officials looking grief-stricken. When we went closer we discovered that the king of the territory lay dead amidst weeping attendants. The Ācārya then turned to me and said in a low voice, "Dear Padmapāda, I have an idea. This is the body of King Amaruka, a very noble ruler. A hundred wives of his are back in the palace who do not yet know of this sad news. The king came here hunting yesterday and seems to have died overnight owing perhaps to heart disease. This may be a good opportunity for me to enter his body in spirit through a yogic process which I learnt in my childhood.

"Then I can be among the women, in the body of the king and learn all about the art of love at firsthand. I will thus be able to excel Bhāratī even in the knowledge of *Kāma Śāstra* and have Maṇḍana as my disciple. There is no need to worry about the *sannyāsin's* vow of celibacy because my love experiences will be confined to the king's body and no sin ever attaches to the spirit. While I exist in the king's body, you will keep my body in safe custody so that I can return and repossess it."

Frankly, I was worried about this proposal of the Ācārya's, not because of moral considerations for what he had said about the sinlessness of the spirit was absolutely true, but because of practical problems. I ventured to convey my feelings. "Sir, there is nothing that I know that you are not aware of yourself. You are omniscient. Yet my devotion to you compels me to express my misgivings about your plan. I am concerned about the likely effects of the company of women, who are wiles incarnate, on you. It is easy to get entangled in the pleasures of the senses but hard to get out of. The great sage Vyāsa says that even an ascetic is susceptible to female charm. And we know from the epics that in ancient times Yogī Matsyendra, desirous of helping the people of the realm, entered the dead body of the king and began to rule benevolently. Because of his greatness, rains came on time, crops multiplied, people forgot their mutual animosities, and peace and prosperity prevailed everywhere. After some time, the king's ministers suspected that there was a change in their king's attitude and actions which were now those of a saint. With a view to retaining the new spirit permanently in the king's body, they encouraged his queens to use all their amorous skills and keep him totally absorbed in love games. Matsyendra gradually got involved in sense pleasures forgetting his saintly nature. Sex became more important than *samādhi*, women more absorbing than Viṣṇu.

"Now his disciple Gorakṣa, a very devoted man who was guarding his body, began to wonder why his teacher had not returned on the stipulated day. He then entered the palace in the guise of a dance instructor and gained access to the king. In subtle ways he redirected the king's attention to Vedānta and succeeded with difficulty in bringing him back into his own body. I have mentioned this episode only to express my fears and not to question your decision. Please forgive me if I have transgressed any propriety of behavior."

The Ācārya understood my concern. "Dear Padmapāda, you have spoken well and nothing needs to be forgiven. You see, it was Matsyendra's own karma that dragged him down the slippery slopes of sensuality. When his karma was exhausted, he was rescued. The other side of the picture is that a yogi who has mastered the technique of *vajrolī* to control his vital functions can remain celibate even though he has sexual relations with a hundred women. We have the example of Kṛṣṇa the Arch-Yogī who lived with eight wives and sixteen thousand shepherdesses. So also in my case. I will be unaffected even though I appear to be submerged in *samsāra*. To me world does not exist except as a dream. To me this body is unreal; it has no connection with the *ātman*. The scriptural injunctions apply only to those who wallow in ignorance and believe that the body is the Self. No karma attaches to me because it will all be like dream activity.

"Neither good nor evil exists for one who realizes that everything is a reflection of Brahman and there is nothing apart from Brahman, just as there is no pot apart from the clay it is made of. The Upaniṣads tell us that when Indra offered the bodies of a thousand ascetics to the wolves not a hair on his body was harmed. Though King Janaka performed a thousand sacrifices, he never had to reincarnate to enjoy the results. Because of his realization of the Self, he was constantly enjoying its bliss, no matter what he did. Similarly, even if I appear to be indulging in sense gratification, no evil will come out of it. I don't even have to change bodies but for the fact that I do not want to appear to be setting a bad example to other *sannyāsins*."

Upon hearing these words of great wisdom, I realized my folly in trying to advise a realized soul. We then moved to a distant mountain cave where the Ācārya instructed us on the safekeeping of his body after he left it. Then he sat in the lotus posture, closed his eyes, and arrested his breath We saw a light emanate from his heart and move toward the dead king. It entered his body and the king, thus quickened, slowly opened his eyes and saw his weeping attendants and officials. They were now quite relieved to see their king alive. He must have had a temporary loss of consciousness which they mistook for death. With great glee the hunting party returned to the palace where it announced its arrival with pomp and ceremony.

The officials narrated to the court the whole series of events and how they almost gave up the king for dead. They announced three days of festivities throughout the kingdom to mark the king's revival and performed other propitiatory rites as thanksgiving to the gods that restored his life. The Ācārya began to rule the land dispensing divine justice To the queens he was like the god of love himself. He was unsurpassed when giving to the needy, unrivalled in valor when dealing with rebellious neighbors, and unequalled in his power of speech in literary discussions with the court poets. The groves and orchards bore abundant fruit. Cows yielded plentiful milk, and the rains produced bumper crops. There was no trace of enmity or disaffection in any corner of the realm. Sickness and disease disappeared altogether. All these did not happen before Amaruka's revival in the forest.

The wise ministers therefore suspected that the spirit that now animated the king's body must belong to a mahātmā. The king really died in the forest. It did not matter whoever was inside his body now, but it was important to keep that spirit there for the good of the people.

The ministers did not of course know that the new king also spent a good deal of his time in the harem disporting himself to his satisfaction and that of its matchless inmates. He played dice with the women and won the wager which was always some sexual favor or other. He drank wine from golden goblets with them and then derived the full benefit of their inebriation. He kissed them and hugged their soft bodies which resembled slender vines. He crushed their bosoms against his bare chest and was surprised that the more he hurt them the more they begged to be hurt. The more love they had the more they hungered for it. They enjoyed the king's rejuvenation to the fullest, while the Ācārya in him learnt the lessons in practical love with great rapidity. The quicker he grasped a point, the quicker they moved on to the next, and the next. The sex education of the Ācācya was complete in no time at all. During this time, he even produced a well-known treatise on sex called *Amaruka* in just three days. After all, the Ācārya had always been a quick learner!

With the Ācārya away in the palace, days passed slowly and painfully for all of us. Some of my friends began to wonder whether the Ācārya remembered about his body and the disciples he left behind. I tried to allay their fears as best I could, telling them he would return soon. A few more days went by. Toward the evening one day one of the newer disciples returned to the cave with the news that the king's ministers had ordered the seizure and destruction of all uncremated bodies. This definitely posed a threat for us.

The king's soldiers would soon discover the Ācārya's body and we would all be in trouble. So I told a few of my friends that we should go into the palace the next morning and remind the Ācārya-in-Amaruka to return forthwith to his own body. Having heard that musicians are allowed to go into the inner palace where the king now spent most of his time, we decided to don the garbs of folksingers to achieve our goal.

We carried out our plan in the morning and met the king. He was shining like the very sun in a silk robe hemmed in gold. Women of rare beauty surrounded him in admiration, their eyes like half-open lotuses and their complexion that of roses. The great hall was filled with the fragrance of exotic flowers and incense. Some women were dancing, others singing, yet others playing a variety of instruments that produced languorous notes. The very air was filled with desire. It took us a minute to tear ourselves from this sensuous vision. The king did not see us; if he did, he did not recognize us. He was too busy romancing a few younger residents of the facility to pay attention to some poor musicians. Failing to catch his eye in the first attempt, we began to sing, after a young woman had just finished an amorous lyric which sent the king into raptures.

"O Illustrious Amaruka, please accept the humble salutations of your old friends. We are your subjects, so we are your friends. A king is like a father to all, so we are your children. A king is like a guru to his people, so we are your disciples. Pray look at your disciples who have come from yonder hills. We went to the hill in search of a cave and, lo, we found a body in the cave. The body is ignorance, the cave is ignorance. Ignorance surrounded by ignorance, O Great Teacher. You are the teacher of teachers. Pray tell us how we can get rid of our ignorance, this body consciousness. How can we realize ourselves, the self in all of us, the Self in you? The Vedas tell us that all this is *Brahman*, all this is Bliss Supreme. But we ignorant fools are interested in guarding the body, because we think it is important. It might be in danger, who knows? How can we develop that great discrimination by which we negate all physical appearance and get to the Self? We desperately need your guidance. We desperately need you. Please guide us by the hand. Please come with us. Help us get away from the cave of ignorance."

The wise Ācārya did not need all these subtle references to his mission. He was indeed keeping track of time. The only thing he did not know was that the ministers had ordered the destruction of his body. At any rate, since his disciples seemed very concerned that he should return to his body, by a reversal of the original yogic process, he entered it right away. And not a minute too soon, either, because the soldiers had already discovered it and just set fire to it, when the few disciples who were guarding it all left together for their morning ablutions. As a result, the Ācārya's right hand sustained severe burns. It was however restored to its normal health when the Ācārya prayed to Lord Narasiṁha asking him for a helping hand and support. Our joy knew no bounds at this reunion. No lovers ever took separation more seriously to heart than we did.

Now the Ācārya was fully prepared to face Bhāratī in any debate on the art of love. So we all rushed back to town to meet her and fulfill the Ācārya's promise. It was exactly thirty days since we left. Maṇḍana was very pleased to see the Ācārya. Unlike the first time he met him, he welcomed him with full honors and bowed to his feet.

He declared that he was ready to renounce the world, his possessions, and his wife.

Bhāratī, who stood by her husband's side, spoke with much humility. "O renowned teacher of humanity, there is no need of any further debate on any subject. You are the acknowledged master of all learning in the three worlds. I know that you could have easily defeated me thirty days ago if you wanted to, but you felt that it was improper to do so. You resemble Lord Śiva, the destroyer of the god of love, in your asceticism but in your knowledge of physical love, you are the god of love himself. So the question of my challenging you does not arise. For one who is the master of the lore of Brahman itself, mundane lore is nothing. My intention in broaching the subject at all was to let the world know that the winner of the debate with the indefatigable Maṇḍana was indeed the master of all learning.

"It is no degradation to be beaten in argument by such a unique person. My husband will now accept *sannyāsa* and will be your disciple. I am proud to have had such a great scholar for my husband. Now that you have considered him fit to be your disciple, I am even more proud. I am not surprised that things have transpired this way. From what little knowledge I had of astrology, I knew even before my marriage that I would one day lose him to a great ascetic. I shall now return to my parents' place and devote the rest of my life to study and meditation. It is strange that you came to beg for a debate and received the debater himself as alms."

Maṇḍana gave away all his property to the poor and bade his noble wife goodbye. The Ācārya praised the gracious lady for her sacrifice and her great wisdom. He now fulfilled Kumārila Bhaṭṭa's wish that he should add the learned Maṇḍana to his fold. He took him to the river and, in waist-deep water, imparted in his ear one of the four great declarations, *tat tvam asi.* The new disciple was christened Sureśvara.

15

MAṆḌANA'S ONE LAST DOUBT

While Maṇḍana was convinced of the irrefutable truth of the Ācārya's argument and the unshakability of his position, he still had one nagging doubt in the back of his mind. He wanted to have it cleared before he left with the Ācārya. How could the great Jaimini, the founder of the ritualistic school, place action above knowledge? The Ācārya had just established beyond the shadow of a doubt that knowledge of the Self was the ultimate goal of man. Could the Ācārya kindly enlighten him on this point?

The Ācārya was very sympathetic. He began to explain the problem with much insight. "Learned Maṇḍana, what you have raised is a legitimate question, especially in view of the fact that both Jaimini, the ritualist, and Vyāsa, the *advaitin*, base their arguments on Vedic statements. Interestingly, too, Jaimini was a disciple of Vyāsa. The answer to the apparent contradiction between ritualism based on a dualistic conception of existence and the non-dual approach must be sought in our limited understanding of the cryptic statements of great sages like Jaimini.

"You see, sages and prophets across the ages have geared their teachings to their time, clime, and society. They have propounded the truth in such a way as to be acceptable to their publics, given a certain amount of understanding and living under certain social and political conditions. Not that there has ever been a fragmentation of the One Truth, but the people could comprehend only certain aspects of it. So, too, in the case of Jaimini. There is no irreconcilable difference between him and the non-dualistic perception of Reality."

The even tenor of the Ācārya's explanation continued. "Jaimini knew very well that the ordinary people could not aspire for a sudden dawning of knowledge, they wallowed in *samsāra*. They needed something that would give them support, something that they could fit into their daily routine. It was easier for them to believe that there was a god different from them to whom they could offer sacrifices and who would grant them their prayers for children, happiness, wealth, etc. This was all right, mind you, because a section of the Vedas does endorse the efficacy of the rituals and sacrifices. But in the later parts, they point out the transitoriness even of heaven and the gods that inhabit it. The real effect of rituals on the performer however is that they *prepare* him for self-inquiry and acquisition of *Brahman* knowledge. As soon as he realizes the nature of the Self, he automatically drops all action for the sake of fruit."

Maṇḍana interrupted. "If Jaimini accepted the Vedas as positing an ever-existing *Brahman*, birthless and deathless, why did he propound that karma is in itself capable of yielding fruit?"

"There is nothing wrong with that, for every action has its fruit even as every cause has its effect, whether we perceive it or not. That is why, in fact, Jaimini said that there is no need for a god to create the world or to destroy it. The world, in the highest conception, is self-generating and self-destroying, being rooted in action. The world ceases to exist for one who has transcended action, because he knows it only as a shadow of *Brahman* which is himself."

Maṇḍana was greatly relieved to hear this explanation. Now he did not have to disown the founder of his school. However, to make absolutely certain that he was not being talked into a compromising position, he prayed to the sage Jaimini for verification. He received the necessary support in a vision. "Dear Maṇḍana, what the young Ācārya told you is correct. It is also the whole truth. How could I view the Vedas differently from the revered Vyāsa who was my own guru? Brahman *is* the ultimate Reality. Karma is only a *means* to that end. Therefore set your mind at rest and follow the great ascetic for a fuller understanding of the here and the hereafter."

Before we left off the subject, the Ācārya made up a few verses commending the carefree nature of the life of the *sannyāsin* as opposed to that of the married man. "Happy indeed is one who has only a loin cloth for his wealth, the begging bowl in his hand, and the supreme utterances of the Vedas on his mind. Sitting under a tree and sustaining his body with a meager morsel, he feels like an emperor. Having totally controlled desires, he enjoys the bliss within."

16
THE PRIMITIVE KĀPĀLIKA

After the defeat of Maṇḍana Miśra and his conversion to *advaita*, the Ācārya proposed that we travel south. Walking with him through forest and desert and over hills and plains was always a great pleasure. There was nothing like learning about this world and beyond in the peripatetic mode, particularly in the company of a great teacher like the Ācārya who was considerate of our physical as well as philosophic well-being. He would relate to us stories from the Vedas and the Upaniṣads and ask us about their import. He would never ridicule anyone's opinion, but would point out a better approach to the problem at hand. Even though we all knew our own individual branches of learning, he knew them *all* and could answer any question on any one of them. For an ascetic, he had a great sense of humor and would enjoy a joke as well as the rest of us.

The places that the Ācārya chose to visit either had hallowed shrines or well-known scholars of one or the other of the dualistic schools. On the way he would stop at the smaller centers of pilgrimage and hold discussions. If anybody argued, he would respond with ruthless logic until the opponent surrendered. He would never himself have any ill will toward hostile religious sects but they did not always reciprocate his charity of understanding. In fact, the more ridiculous their attitude, the more forgiving he was. An incident that took place at our next stop bore testimony to this.

After traveling many, many days we reached a large river whose waters were clear and whose banks were lined with fruit trees of various kinds. The gentle fragrance of the flowers which grew in abundance wafted in the breeze soothing one's body and mind. We all felt like resting there for some time. Even before we suggested that, the Ācārya announced that we reached the famous town of Śrī Śailam with an age-old Śiva temple known for its beauty as well as its potency. The holy hill on which the temple was located was known as Indra Kīla. It was the location of a fierce battle between Lord Śiva and Arjuna the Pāṇḍava. Śiva, who was pleased with Arjuna's fairness and determination in battle, blessed him and gave him access to an indestructible weapon through a special mantra which later helped him in the epic war of succession with the Kauravas described in the *Mahābhārata.* We worshipped at the temple and sojourned in the neighborhood for some time.

In the vicinity of Śrī Śailam there lived a primitive tribe of Kālī-worshippers called Kāpālikas. They were so named for the necklace of human skulls that they wore. According to their belief, human sacrifice to their goddess would ensure them benefits. The kind of benefits they were supposed to derive depended upon the greatness of the person sacrificed.

Since these barbarians had nothing like a philosophy, the Ācārya had no trouble at all proving that their superstitions were silly. He also suggested a more humane form of Kālī worship without involving any sacrifice, human or animal. The leader of the sect was not very happy about this turn of events for he would lose his control over the tribe once the superstition was destroyed. So he wanted to get rid of the Ācārya. Since he knew that this would not be possible when the Ācārya was surrounded by his disciples, he decided to se guile. Accordingly, one afternoon when the

Ācārya was resting after the lesson, he approached him in the guise of an ascetic.

"Noblest among ascetics, having heard a great deal about your greatness, scholarship, omniscience, and pure life, I have come to you to make a rather strange request. You are a great teacher of non-dualism. Moreover, you practice what you teach, every letter of it. I have also heard of your merciful nature. You are the most virtuous among men. It is impossible to find so many great qualities in any one person. Owing to my great good fortune I am able to meet you in person. *Advaitins* like you, though they are themselves not involved in the world, live for the sake of others. They do not attach any importance to their bodies, looking upon them as bags of bones and flesh, blood and excrement. They are ready to give them up any moment if it serves the people in any way. Now, let me mention my problem to you and beseech your help.

"For many years, I performed austerities in the jungle to obtain a vision of Bhairava who appeared to me at last. When I expressed my desire to be transported into heaven in my physical form to enjoy the good life, he told me that in order to achieve that objective I would have to offer the head of a great king or ascetic on the altar. I have so far not been able to find any such person and, when I saw you, my hopes began to blossom again. If you will let me have your head, I can attain my desire and you will go down in history as one who made the ultimate sacrifice for the sake of another. Please do no deny me this favor, I beg of you. You have anyway disconnected your soul from your body. For a person who has eschewed all desire, what use is the body except remain a great burden?"

The Ācārya did not find anything strange in this request. Nor did he have any reason to suspect the genuineness of the requestor. After all, he knew that in certain kinds of primitive worship human sacrifice was made, though he always condemned it. So he not only agreed to the request without any hesitation because it would help the desperate Kāpālika but also suggested a plan to carry out the sacrifice. During the day, he would be in the company of his disciples, so he promised to come to the Bhairava temple in the dead of night undetected by anyone. Then he could offer his head to the deity.

The Kāpālika was very pleased that he would be able to wreak vengeance on the Ācārya who effectively disbanded his tribe. When it was around midnight, the Ācārya quietly slipped out of the camp and proceeded to fulfill his promise to the Kāpālika. The Kāpālika was ready with his machete for the sacrifice, and the preliminary rites were already in progress.

At about this time I happened to look in the direction of where the Ācārya had been sleeping. I always thought of him, and had nothing but his welfare on my mind all the time. Maybe I had a premonition that something was wrong. Maybe I was worried about him because in debating contests he had made too many enemies. Where could he have gone by himself in the middle of the night? I began to get suspicious and angry at the same time. In extreme anger I imagined myself to be a man-lion, just like Lord Narasiṁha, and decided to tear any would-be assailant of the Ācārya limb from limb. I am not sure of the exact sequence of events at this point, but when it was all over my friends told me what happened. I roared my way through the dense forest to the temple with most of them behind me in panic, not knowing what the matter was and where I was headed.

I directly went into the sanctum of the temple where the Ācārya was in a trance with all his senses withdrawn into the mind and the mind into the spirit looking like a dead person. I was mad with rage to see the Kāpālika with a deadly sword in his upraised hands just about to decapitate the Ācārya. In a trice I jumped on his back and struck him to the ground. Then with my sharp claws and fangs, I proceeded to eviscerate him on the spot, excited by his very cries of agony. I did not stop until I dumped the shreds of his body in the pool of his own blood on the floor.

After this event I remained dazed for a while during which time the Ācārya recovered his normal consciousness. When I regained my faculties, I saw the Ācārya tending me with loving concern. The awesome carcass of the Kāpālika was by his side. My friends were extremely grateful to me for saving the life of our beloved teacher. They plied me with questions as to how I was able to fell the mighty Kāpālika. I then narrated to them the story of how I came to possess the power to assume Narasiṁha consciousness.

"As a young boy I was very fascinated by the concept of God as man-lion. To understand its mystery, I began to meditate on it for a long time. I removed myself to a cave on a hillside for the purpose. After some time, a hunter who watched me practice severe austerities asked me what I desired to accomplish. I told him that I wanted to have a vision of Narashiṁha who was known to be very gracious to his devotees. Then he said, 'Why do you take so much trouble to see one who is right here on the hill? You wait here, I will bring him to you.' He disappeared into the trees and emerged back a little later with someone tied with a vine walking slowly behind him. On closer examination, I found that this was Lord Narasiṁha. Prostrating myself before Him in utter astonishment, I asked the Lord why he who was impossible to be seen even by great sages was content to be bound by an ordinary hunter.

"In a thunderous voice the Lord said, 'The great sages do not have the kind of devotion that this man has for me. Know that I am easily bound by devotion. I respond to sincere appeals. I am pleased with you, and will help you when you need me. Just call my name and you will be possessed of my qualities and will be able to accomplish what you wish.' He then blessed the hunter and me and disappeared."

Upon hearing this story, the Ācārya and my friends began to pray to Lord Narasiṁha and presently I too joined them in offering my gratitude to the benevolent god.

17

HASTĀMALAKA JOINS THE FOLD

In our tours we once passed through a village called Śrī Bali where we begged our food for the noon. The village was unique in many ways. Two thousand brahmins lived there in perfect harmony, each content with performing his duties and tending the sacrificial fire. The chanting of the Vedas could be heard above the laughter of playing children and the chirping of the birds. The people were truthful, kind, and hospitable. No premature or violent deaths had ever been known to take place there.

A wealthy brahmin of the village, Prabhākara by name, had a seven-year old son who was mute and retarded. His behavior was totally idiotic. He ate if someone fed him, slept when someone laid him down. He did nothing on his own. He did not play or want to study. He was not annoyed when other children played pranks on him or even when they beat him. Prabhākara had heard that the Ācārya revived a dead child just by looking at him in a nearby village. He knew that sages and *sannyāsins* had great powers and were able to control the very elements. So he decided to try his luck. He brought the boy to the tree where we were resting after lunch. Prostrating himself before the Ācārya, he related his problem and prayed for help. The boy also was asked to kneel. He did so but continued in that position, refusing to get up.

The father spoke in anguish. "Though he is seven years old, this boy has not yet learned the alphabet. He does not care for instruction. He is not interested in anything at all. His mother and I are very worried about him. We hope that you can enlighten us on the cause of the boy's condition. We will be grateful to you forever."

The Ācārya sympathetically listened to the man, and asked the boy a few simple questions to gage the level of his comprehension. "Who are you, my child? What are your interests? You have a cheerful face, but you act like a vegetable. Won't you talk to me and tell me about yourself?"

To the surprise of all of us, and particularly the dumbfounded Prabhākara, the boy responded to the Ācārya in a dozen beautiful verses. "O Teacher of the world, I am by no means an insentient being. Not only that, by association with me, all beings become sentient. I am that undivided Self which is beyond the six states and six conditions, beyond caste and creed, body and mind, thought and intuition. I am that ultimate illuminer of all, the *Ātman*, that is the basis of all existence. I am the ever-abiding Awareness which manifests itself to those who have suppressed their minds and transcended their desires. I am the witness of all that happens in all three worlds, yet I am not involved in anything. I am the meaning of all existence. I am Bliss."

The Ācārya knew at once that this boy was no idiot and that the abnormality of his behavior was only apparent. He placed his hands on the boy's head and blessed him. Then turning to Prabhākara he said, "By virtue of his past actions, your son has acquired profound spiritual wisdom though no one taught him anything in this life. He just acts dumb because he is interested in nothing in this world except to remain within himself . He does not wish to be bothered with any worldly activity. Now, under these circumstances, he will be no help to you or anyone else in the family. So can you leave him with me?"

Prabhākara was happy that his apparently retarded son was an enlightened soul, but he was reluctant to let him go with the Ācārya as a *sannyāsin.* He did not know what to say. Noting his hesitation the Ācārya spoke in a reassuring voice, "Prabhākara, perhaps I can help you make up your mind by narrating an incident in this boy's life which you may remember. When the boy was three, you and your wife took him along with you to a lake where you wanted to bathe. You left him alone lakeside and went into the water. While you were engrossed in your ablutions, he slowly toddled to the edge and fell into the lake. When you came out of the lake, you saw the lifeless body of the boy in the water and were disconsolate. As it turned out, a yogī who was meditating nearby saw what happened. Being very kind-hearted, he gave up his own body and entered into that of your son. That was when you must have started noticing the change in him. So it is actually a yogī who inhabits the body of your son."

Convinced that he really had lost his son several years before, Prabhākara left the boy in the Ācārya's care. Since the twelve verses that the boy composed in answer to the question "who are you?" present the greatest philosophy in an easy-to-understand manner, just like the berry *āmalaka* in one's palm is easily visible and readily consumable, he came to be known as Hastāmalaka. We all welcomed him enthusiastically into our group though he continued to ignore his surroundings most of the time. We knew from that vacant look on his face that he was much ahead of us in spiritual knowledge and experience.

18
THE FOURTH DISCIPLE, TOṬAKA

After the addition of Hastāmalaka to our fold, we moved further south to Śṛṅgerī, the place that had earlier impressed the Ācārya with its natural beauty and serenity on his first outward passage from home. The river Tuṅga flowed in the vicinity adding a great deal of charm to the area.

There for a while the Ācārya taught his philosophy to the people helping them understand the principles of right knowledge and discrimination. He thought that it would be a good idea to have a temple built in the heart of the town which could serve as a center of culture and learning. He accomplished this objective with the help of the local ruler and the merchants. He invoked the presence of Sarasvatī, the goddess of learning, in the temple and gave her the popular name Śāradā. This was the origin of the famous mission which the Ācārya was to establish later.

During the festivities in connection with the dedication of the temple, a brahmin approached the Ācārya with his palms folded in humility. He stood there with bent head until the Ācārya noticed him and asked him what he wanted. The brahmin said in simple Sanskrit, "Venerable Sir, my name is Giri. Some also call me Udaṅka, son of Śīlada. I am a poor man from this town without any attachments or obligations. I am illiterate and therefore cannot spend my time reading the *śāstras*. I am not initiated into any spiritual practice, so I do not know anything about it. I cannot engage in trade because I have no money. But I have a desire to lead a useful life in the service of a great personage. I know of no greater person than you. On seeing you, I feel a great sense of peace overcome me.

"I notice that, although you have many great and scholarly disciples, there is none in your entourage to perform the menial jobs that need to be done. So please grant me that privilege. I will wash your clothes, sweep the campsite, and clean your water pots. Please do not deny me this favor."

The Ācārya was quite touched by Giri's humble appeal, and consented for him to be his personal attendant, even though he did not need one. Every day Giri would wake up before the master, wash his clothes, sweep the floor, and make all the arrangements for the master's ablutions. He would anticipate all his needs. He would walk behind him like his very shadow. When the class started, he would stand at a respectful distance with folded hands. While waiting attentively for his master's pleasure, he would listen to the lessons and feel sad that he did not have the intelligence to understand them. Yet he felt that he was on top of the world because he had the unique privilege of serving the greatest ācārya in the world.

This relationship between Giri and the Ācārya continued for some time. One day the class assembled as usual and recited the invocatory verses. The Ācārya, instead of commencing the lesson, waited looking hither and thither. When the class still did not start after some time, I got a little impatient and asked the Ācārya whether he was expecting someone. He said, "Yes, Giri is not here yet. He must have been delayed somewhere." The other disciples and I were very surprised to hear this because we never regarded the illiterate Giri as part of the class, let alone as one worth waiting for. I said as much aloud, "Sir, it is strange that you are holding up the class for the sake of the errand boy. What good will it do him, anyway, to join us for he won't understand a syllable of what is going on here? One might as well teach a pillar or a post."

"Yes, Padmapāda, Giri is like a pillar or a post when it comes to understanding our lessons. But he is a great listener, so I thought I'd wait for him." I did not understand what the Ācārya meant, but I remained silent not daring to ask for further clarification.

While this exchange was going on, Giri was washing the clothes in the river. The Ācārya felt great pity for him who was the epitome of service. He closed his eyes for a few minutes and thought of the devoted Giri. At the same time Giri had a great feeling of joy penetrate his being. He suddenly received a charge of knowledge and power from the master. He came running to the Ācārya with the wet clothes on his arms. He knelt in front of him with redoubled humility and with new confidence, sang his praise in erudite Sanskrit, tears rolling down his cheeks.

"Best of all preceptors, you are the great knower of all *śāstras* and the embodiment of Truth. You are an ocean of grace and mercy. In it please submerge this mountain of ignorance. You shine like the sun among scholars; there is none who can equal you in learning. Yet you are within reach of people like me who surrender to you. I seek refuge at your feet even though I lack the qualifications even to wear their dust on my head."

He composed eight impromptu verses in the melodious *toṭaka* meter. The beauty and structure of each was such that I was speechless with disbelief, and so were my friends in the class. The Ācārya turned to me and smiled as if asking me, "Well, what do you think of the pillar now?" I was quite ashamed of my behavior in front of the class. While the others were still trying to figure out what happened, the Ācārya graciously explained.

"You see, gentlemen, besides scholarship it is important to cultivate the quality of faith in spiritual endeavor. Through faith you will have concentration of the mind. It will then become pure and ready to receive instruction." We had known by then that it was the master's grace that descended on Giri and salvaged him from the depths of ignorance. But in order to deserve that extraordinary kindness, he had the requisite faith in the master and the spirit of selfless devotion and service. The Ācārya then blessed him and conferred on him the new name of Toṭaka in recognition of his delightful poem.

19
A CLASS SESSION ON BRAHMAN

We began this class session with the *śānti mantra:*

pūrṇamadaḥ pūrṇamidam
pūrṇāt pūrṇamudacyate
pūrṇasya pūrṇamādāya
pūrṇamev āvaśiṣyate

That is whole, this is whole. From the whole, the whole is manifested. With the whole taken out of the whole, the whole remains.

A few minutes of silence. The Ācārya began in his sonorous voice. "I told you that the knowledge of the Self is the right knowledge. In this context, let me recount to you what the great sage Yājñavalkya said to his wife: 'Dear Maitreyī, I am about to renounce the state of the householder and go to the forest for meditation. Before I do so I'd like to divide my property between you and my other wife Kātyāyanī.'

"Then Maitreyī said, 'Venerable Sir, what should I do with that which does not make me immortal? Tell me, sir, about what you know of immortality.'

"Then the sage responded. 'You were dear to me before. Now you are even dearer for you have asked me a wise question. Listen carefully. A wife is dear to her husband not because she is the wife but because she is the Self. So, too, the husband to the wife, the son to the father, the father to the son. Therefore the Self should be seen, heard of, meditated upon.

"Now let me tell you about the Bliss of *Brahman.* The greatest happiness known to humans is being healthy, wealthy, and powerful. The bliss of the *pitṛs* is a hundred times this bliss. The bliss of the demigods is a hundred times that of the *pitṛs*. The bliss of one who is versed in the Vedas, without sin, and is not affected by desire is a hundred times that of the demigods. A thousand times the bliss of the sinless and desireless Vedic scholar may give you some idea of the bliss of *Brahman.* The best of mortals therefore enjoys but a tiny fraction of that Infinite Bliss, dear Maitreyī.' Maitreyī was very pleased and received Brahman instruction from Yājñavalkya. The other wife settled for the vast property."

The Ācārya continued. "*Brahman* is effulgence, the Great Fire. The universe is filled with fire. The god of rain is fire, the year is the fuel, clouds are the smoke, lightning the flame, thunder the sparks. In the fire the gods offer *soma*. Out of the sacrifice comes the rain.

"This world is fire, the earth is the fuel, the night the smoke, and the stars the sparks. The gods offer rain in this fire, and food is produced.

"The man is fire, his open mouth the fuel, vital breath the smoke, speech the flame, and the eyes the sparks. In this fire the gods offer food, and semen is produced.

"The woman is fire, her vulva the fuel, the hair smoke, the sheath the flame, intromission the coals, and joy the sparks. In this fire the gods offer semen, and out of this offering arises the person. Thus all is fire. All is *Brahman*."

The Ācārya paused and looked at us as if inviting questions. I asked the first question, "Learned Ācārya, how does one know that the Self or *Brahman* exists at all?" The Ācārya smiled benignly. "Padmapāda, you can answer that question yourself. Just think for a minute. When you asked me the question, who was it really that asked it? Every time you say 'I' who is saying it? Any time you refer to yourself, you are really referring to your Self, not the body. The Self in everyday parlance appears as 'I am.' 'I' is the first syllable, the first word. The word is sound. Sound is the modification of Silence. And Silence is *Brahman*. To deny one's self is to deny one's existence. How can there be any question regarding this fundamental fact?"

"Could you explain it further, please? How am I as the Self different from the objects that I perceive?"

"Let's look at the question logically. The object is the perceived and the eye the perceiver. But the eye itself may be said to be the perceived because the mind perceives through the eye. The mind in turn is subject to so many modifications and states that the ultimate perceiver has to be different from it. It is this ultimate perceiver, this witness of all, that is the Self. You first exist, that is, you are; and then you think, see, do, etc., and not the other way around.

"This power that exists, this consciousness, neither dawns nor disappears, neither increases nor decreases. It is self-shining and illuminates all other faculties. The other faculties are in themselves inert but appear to be conscious in conjunction with the Self. This relationship is similar to that of fire and the hot iron ball. As long as the heat permeates the ball it looks and feels hot. We cannot separate the heat from the metal. Again, the shape of the red hot metal can be changed any way we like but the heat itself is unaffected because it has no form. Another example is the relationship of water to the waves and the foam. Water is the substratum; the waves and the foam are only manifestations. There is no higher knowledge or bliss than *Brahman*."

Then Sureśvara asked the question that was uppermost in all our minds. "How does one realize Brahman?"

"There are some preliminary qualifications. One has to be totally detached in mind, and possess discrimination of what is permanent and what is transient, control of the body and the senses and, most importantly, a yearning for liberation.

"A seeker of Truth should look upon the world as the droppings of a crow and turn away from all its attractions, understanding that they are unreal and evanescent. He should cultivate tolerance toward pain and sorrow. These are the negative steps.

"Then there are some positive steps. You must know that knowledge cannot be acquired without inquiry. So you must constantly inquire who you are, how you and this world came into being, who its maker is, etc. The greatest delusion that the human being suffers from is that the body is the same as *ātman*. There cannot be greater stupidity than such thinking. *Ātman* is indivisible, pure, eternal; the body consists of many parts and is subject to decay. Just as a person going in a boat feels that the world around him is swaying, just as everything appears yellow to the jaundiced eye, just as a mirage is mistaken for water, and just as the moon appears to be moving when the clouds are moving, so too the body appears to be *ātman*. But after the dawn of *Brahman* consciousness, this delusion disappears, just as upon close examination a coil of rope is seen for what it really is and not the serpent that it has been mistaken to be.

"The wise use the phenomenal world only as a means of inferring the principle behind it. Once that intelligent principle has been grasped, they have no more use for it."

The class was then dismissed with the suggestion that we should churn these things over in our minds.

20
BICKERING AMONG THE DISCIPLES

The ācārya now spent some quiet time in Śṛṅgerī paying much attention to his disciples. Sureśvara, Hastā malaka, and Toṭaka had now become fully established in our group and were helping the Ācārya in many ways in the propagation of *advaita.* The Ācārya, I had reason to believe, was also pleased with my services. In order to facilitate the furtherance of our mission, it was felt that an exegesis of the Ācārya's commentary might be useful to the scholars. The question then was who should be entrusted with the task.

Sureśvara was desirous of proving his total loyalty to the Ācārya and commitment to his teachings at the first opportunity. So he approached the Ācārya and asked to be allowed to do the exegesis on the *Brahma Sūtra* commentary. "I am sure I am not competent to understand all the mysteries of the great science of the Self as developed by you. But if I have your grace I can easily accomplish the task." The Ācārya readily agreed to the proposal, happy that his own commentary would now have a larger readership. However I was not very happy with this proposal. Neither were the other disciples too keen on Sureśvara going through with the project. After all, was not this Sureśvara a staunch ritualist until recently? Just because he was defeated in debate by the Ācārya and, abiding by the rules of the contest, he became a *sannyāsin*, was there any guarantee that he changed overnight? What if he interpreted the Ācārya's teachings in the wrong light and the *advaita* ideal was compromised?

When I expressed my misgivings to the Ācārya, he did not say anything. I went on, "Why not ask

Hastāmalaka to do the job? Or Toṭaka, who just proved to be worthy of your grace? Or if you think I have the competence, I shall attempt it. But we all feel that Sureśvara would be the wrong choice, if I may be so bold as to speak my mind." The Ācārya said, "I understand your concern. I thought Sureśvara would be the most suitable person for this task because he is very learned and an observer of dharma. But if you are all opposed to the idea, we will forget it. Hastāmalaka is so absorbed in the Self that he might not be interested in any mundane activity. Toṭaka, I believe, derives his satisfaction from serving me and his fellow students in other ways and may not want to undertake any time-consuming academic assignment. You, Padmapāda, are very competent and, if you want to do this work, I certainly will have no objection."

When the Ācārya met Sureśvara alone, he explained the situation to him and said, "Under the circumstances, I think you had better write an independent treatise and bring it to me. Let Padmapāda write the commentary on my work." In accordance with these revised instructions Sureśvara wrote *Naiṣkarmya Siddhi*, a brief but definitive work on how disinterested actions lead one to liberation. This work was shown to all of us. We were very impressed with the beauty of its style and the closeness of its argument. I also produced my book titled *Vijaya Ḍiṇḍima* which the Ācārya thought was unparalleled for its scholarship.

Later I came to know that Sureśvara expressed his displeasure to the Ācārya with the whole proceeding. He seems to have said, "Revered Ācārya, it was not with the intention of gaining name or fame that I offered to work on your commentary. It was only because you commanded me to do it. It is true that as a householder I upheld the ritualist ideal and I even upbraided you for entering my home on the day of the *srāddha*. But I was merely following the custom and the dharma of that stage of my life. If I was antagonistic to *sannyāsa*, why would I let you and your disciples stay as my guests for eighteen days and hold the debate in my house? Further, it is not true that I took to *sannyāsa* because I was defeated in argument by you. It was because I was convinced of the truth and validity of your position. Does it not show that I was open-minded? To give you another example, you saw when you entered my house without notice that I invited *both* Jaimini and Vyāsa. I feel, Sir, that the remarks made by my fellow-disciples were unfair."

The Ācārya saw that Sureśvara was deeply hurt. He consoled him as best he could. I found out that he also told him that, based on the planetary position at the time of the production of my *Vijaya Ḍinḍima,* the book had a bleak future. It would be destroyed except for the first five chapters dealing with the first four *sūtras*. He also foresaw that in a later life Sureśvara would be born as Vācaspati and then fulfill his desire of writing a full-length exposition of his commentary which would attain great popularity.

All of this of course I did not know at the time. But, having reflected on the course of events, I began to feel guilty for the role that I played in this whole episode. I was convinced that I was less than fair to my friend Sureśvara. I had no business questioning the judgment of the Ācārya. The only way to get some peace of mind and perform sort of penance now for me would be to go on a pilgrimage for some time. I decided Rāmeśvaram on the southern tip of the country where the three great seas met would be the ideal place to visit. When I mentioned my plan to the Ācā rya, for some reason he did not seem to be very supportive. He even tried to dissuade me from undertaking the trip. "Padmapāda, why do you want to take all this trouble? It is said that the presence of one's guru confers great benefits and satisfies all desires. Travel is very difficult and is fraught with all kinds of risks. Even if all goes well, you will be constantly worried about your food and lodging, facilities for the daily ablutions, and places for meditation. You won't therefore be able to spend much time on self-inquiry or other spiritual matters. Then there is always the possibility of sickness and, when you are alone, who will look after you? So I suggest that you reconsider your decision."

Since I had already decided to go, I countered his objections. "Please forgive me if I appear to disobey my guru. Though what all you say is correct, I feel that I should go on this trip to regain my mental peace. The *sannyāsin* should not stay in any one place too long lest he should develop an attachment to it. As regards death and diseases, they depend on one's prior karma and cannot be escaped no matter where one is. Daily observances and rites can be attended to, according to the ancient law-givers, in any manner convenient at a given place. And wherever one might be, one who has the guru's grace will be able to enjoy bliss in *samādhi*. During pilgrimages one has a chance of meeting holy people and receiving their blessings, in addition to broadening one's outlook. This will eventually lead one to discrimination which is after all the *sannyāsin* ideal."

Seeing my determination, the Ācārya agreed with what I said and added, "I was merely testing the strength of your resolve. If you feel strongly like going, of course you must go. You have my blessings wherever you go. Now pay attention to my words which you will find useful in your travels. When you travel, always choose the safe and frequented roads and never any byways which are generally used by thieves and thugs. It is also better to go direct to one's destination without tarrying too long on the way. But if you happen to run into good company, you may spend a few days with them. In choosing your companions, don't be misled by the dress or outward appearance or sweet talk. Watch strangers carefully, lest you should find yourself cheated out of the few belongings you have. Above all, never swerve from the path of virtue under any circumstances, and good will befall you."

Overwhelmed by the Ācārya's concern for my well-being, I bowed to his feet and took leave of him.

21
PADMAPĀDA'S TRIP TO RĀMEŚVARAM

As soon as I received the Ācārya's permission I left on my pilgrimage. I first traveled to the famed Śiva temple of Kālahastī and bathed in the holy river, Svarṇamukhī. I then turned south to Kāñcī and Puṇḍarīkapuram both of which also had marvelous temples and rivers. An interesting feature of these temples is that the deity is accompanied by his consort, who is but a form of Primal Energy, Śaktī. In all exploits attributed to Śiva, he was helped by her or advised by her. Then I reached the banks of the Kāverī and worshipped Viṣṇu in the town of Śrīraṅgam. This was a beautiful place to visit and the temple afforded a taste of celestial peace and joy to all who visited it.

From there I proceeded straight to my native village en route to Rāmeśvaram In the village lived my uncle who was glad to see me. A number of other relatives also joined us. Some wept, some joked, others offered salutations as befitted the occasion. They praised me for my decision to lead the life of a *brahmacārin*. That was a sure way of attaining liberation through an understanding of what was permanent and by seeing the one Reality in all. Fortunate indeed were those who took to the staff and deer skin. To them I replied, "It is true that the holy order of *sannyāsa* releases one from a number of avoidable miseries. But it is the straight and narrow path which only a few can traverse successfully. In this life everyone, regardless of their situation, can serve the community. Just as the *sannyāsin* is expected to teach the householder the way to attain Self-knowledge within his own station, the householder is expected to invite the monks and holy men and offer them food. Tradition says that whoever offers food to an ascetic will derive half the merit that the latter has accumulated through his spiritual practices. Besides, the householder can perform the rituals laid down by the scriptures and thereby attain not only his desires but also tranquillity. And if one performs one's duties without any specific motive or desire, one enjoys the bliss of the Self. It is not correct, as is sometimes suggested, to suppose that a householder who fulfills his sensuous desires is not capable of acquiring Self-knowledge or fit for a spiritual life. By a deep understanding of the nature of one's own Self, one gradually sees the wastefulness and the evanescence of those desires and starts looking inward."

My uncle and the other relatives were very pleased with these words. I stayed on at my uncle's home for the midday meal, although a *sannyāsin* was not supposed to get too involved with his relatives. When I was eating my uncle noticed my book dealing with the Ācārya's commentary. He expressed an interest in looking over the work of his ascetic nephew, so I let him read it. As he reviewed the *Vijaya Ḍiṇḍima*, I could sense his appreciation for it which he presently expressed in words. "My dear Sanandana, I am very proud of you. When you left us as a child, I had little idea that you were going to be a fine scholar." He then added, "I see that you and your Ācārya used extremely powerful arguments to refute the logic of the other systems of philosophy. Tell me, do you believe those arguments or did you just advance them for the sake of the argument? Do you think they are valid and conclusive?"

I told him that there was no question of anyone having to *believe* in them or *prove* their validity, because they are self-evident truths which were realized by the sages a thousand times over. The other schools could not say the same thing as their arguments had no experiential proof but were based merely on dry intellection. While my uncle apparently agreed with me, I thought he looked worried. But neither of us said anything about it. In the afternoon, when it was time for me to go, I left a few of my belongings including the *Ḍiṇḍima* behind with my uncle. I thought the journey would be lighter and the book would be safer that way. If there was a glint of mischief in my uncle's eye, I did not notice it. I bade him goodbye saying, "Uncle, I am leaving some of my things with you. I will pick them up on my way back. Please take good care of them for me, especially the book. I cherish it beyond everything else in my life. That is all I have in this world, all my wealth." Upon receiving assurances that no harm would come to the book, I left the village following the road to Rāmeśvaram. My thoughts were already hovering around Śrī Rāma who destroyed the demon Rāvaṇa and restored dharma in Laṅkā. Eventually I approached the sacred town of Rāmeśvaram. I passed through the various hermitages and historic sites where centuries before the great prince had trod as he went in quest of his beloved Sītā. It was in accordance with the advice of the sage Agastya, who had drunk up the entire ocean in a single gulp, that he built the causeway across the sea. In fact the sage offered to repeat his feat, but the wise Rāma prevented him saying that if he accepted his offer people would doubt his own competence. Of course the bridge was no longer there but its starting point, called Setu, was still considered a holy place. It occurred to me that the word "Rāmeśvaram" could refer to one who was the lord of Rāma, one whose lord was Rāma, or Rāma who was the lord of all, depending on its phrasal analysis. Those around me thought it was rather clever. I spent there a few days thinking of the Ācārya and meditating, sitting on the beach hallowed by the waters of the merging seas.

Soon I began to yearn for the company of the Ācārya and my friends. I knew it was time for me to return.

In order to collect the items I left at my uncle's place, I first went to my village. I was surprised to find my uncle distraught with grief. He told me the reason. "Dear nephew, how can I give you the terrible news? Indeed a great misfortune has befallen us. The day after you left I performed the evening *homa* as usual and went to sleep. I was awakened by intense heat and light in the middle of the night. When I awoke, alas, I found the thatched house almost entirely engulfed in flames and my own exit was partially blocked by a burning log. Even so I tried to reach the wooden chest where I kept your book only to find that it was totally burnt. With great difficulty I got out of the house before the roof caved in. I am so grief-stricken that I don't know how to console you. I am very sorry that it was destined that your noble work should not come to light."

I was shocked to hear this. The *Ḍiṇḍima* was my sole possession and I had great hopes for its future. Now nothing was left. Nothing to live for. I was also sorry for my uncle who had lost his house and nearly killed himself trying to save my book. I did not know what to say.

It must be due to my spiritual training that I got out of my depression relatively quickly. Besides, even though I lost the original work, I could still rewrite the whole book. I said as much to my uncle and tried to console him.

My uncle looked very pleased at this possibility and requested me to stay with him for a few more days to recover from my long trip. I agreed to do so. And he began to look after me well, indeed better than the first time. He took particular care of my food, serving me himself with special dishes. I did not know what some of them were or why they tasted strange. But I did not pay much attention. In the meantime, I began to reproduce my work in all seriousness. However, as days went, I found myself unable to recapture the original vitality or inspiration. I also began to feel a little dizzy in my head, so I had to temporarily suspend the project.

In about a week, some of my friends who were also on pilgrimage, happened to come to the village. We were happy to see each other. I made inquiries about the Ācārya's welfare. They also told me about their pilgrimages and the experiences they had. Then they looked at my face and asked me with some concern, "What is wrong, Padmapāda? You look pale. Have you been sick?" Then I told them that I was not particularly sick with any disease, but I did not feel too well for some unexplainable reason. I was not tired. My uncle was taking good care of me. I did not know what was wrong. Anyhow, I expressed a desire to return to the Ācārya at once.

My uncle seemed reluctant to let me go so soon, but we all started in the afternoon on our return journey. On the way we heard about the passing of the Ācārya's mother and that he was waiting for us at a place called Mahāśūrapura. We were all eager to see him after a long separation. The moment we laid eyes on him, we saluted him and repeatedly touched our foreheads to his feet. The Ācārya spoke kindly to us and asked us individually about our experiences and the places that we visited. After we were refreshed, my friends explained my problem to him and wanted to know what was wrong with me. The gracious Ācārya looked intently at me for a minute or so before he spoke.

"There is nothing wrong with Padmapāda. His reason is a bit dimmed owing to a certain slow-acting drug that he was administered along with his food by his uncle. The effect will wear out in a few days and he will be his normal self once again."

My friends and I were very relieved to hear this. But I wondered why my uncle went to such great lengths to drug me. The Ācārya continued, "When Padmapāda showed his *Vijaya Ḍiṇḍima* to his uncle, he pretended to be very pleased with his work. In reality, though he was happy that his nephew was a scholar, he was worried about the content of the work. You see, his uncle is a dualist and is opposed to Vedānta. He knew that if Padmapāda's work was published it would be a severe blow to his doctrines, which he could not tolerate. So he set fire to his own house and made it look like an accident. There is no telling what one does to protect one's religious faith."

He then looked sympathetically at me and consoled me with his heart brimming with affection. "Padmapāda, do not grieve over the loss of your work. No one can escape the effects of past karma. I knew that misfortune would befall you and your work. I told Sureśvara about my fears.

And that was why I tried to discourage you from undertaking your trip. But you wouldn't listen, because you were egged on by destiny, more powerful than I. As regards your work, I can repeat from memory the first five chapters that you read out to me. You can copy them down. The fragment of your work will be known as *Pañcapādikā*. Does that make you feel happy?"

"O Revered Ācārya," I almost cried in my happiness that a part of my work would be saved for posterity, "I am beholden to you beyond words. I am completely in your debt."

22
THE PASSING OF THE MOTHER

Shortly after I left Śṛṅgerī on my pilgrimage, the Ācārya had a sudden uneasy feeling that something was wrong, the details pertaining to which I could gather from my friends only after my return.

The Ācārya reflected on the possible reason for his feelings of unease. His thoughts gradually took him to his aged mother. It occurred to him that she must be nearing her end. He knew that she must be thinking of him, desperately hoping that he would come as promised. He must go and comfort her and help her in her journey into the beyond. Having decided thus, he used a particular yogic technique called *khecarī* which rendered his body weightless, and traveled home through the skies in no time.

The reunion of mother and son was a tearful one. The old lady was overwhelmed with happiness on seeing her son at this critical time. The young ascetic temporarily forgot that in *advaita* there were no mother and son as he wept like an ordinary person. Each quickly regained strength from the sight of the other. The Ācārya, first to recover from his momentary human weakness, asked his mother what her last wish was. The noble lady who had been the wife of a saintly man and the mother of a saint replied, "Dear son, the only desire I had until now was to see you. I have no other desire, certainly none to continue in this decrepit body. If you can, help me have a glimpse of the Reality before my end and put me on the path to my evolution into a higher being."

The Ācārya was very pleased to hear his mother ask for true knowledge. Holding her right hand in his, he directly proceeded with the instruction in Brahman the Unchangeable and the oneness of Consciousness. He emphasized that death was merely the dissolution of the body which was heir to disease and infirmity. The self found for itself a new body as long as there was a balance of karma which in itself was the result of desire. Once desirelessness was achieved, there was no death and no birth. The Law of Karma applied to all beings, humans as well as gods, because everyone was a mutation of the one immutable Brahman. So one should strive to realize it within oneself.

The mother was somewhat uneasy at the end of this learned exposition for she was not familiar with the language or the notion of an abstract being. So she requested her son to produce for her a vision of a benevolent deity with a name and form that she was used to. Since she had been, along with his father, a devotee of Śiva, he chanted a hymn in praise of *Brahman* as Śiva. "I salute to the great Śiva who is eternal, who is the embodiment of knowledge, whose infinite power Brahmā and Viṣṇu tried in vain to comprehend, and who is beyond mind and speech. I bow to the great lord who accommodated his consort in his own body, thus causing confusion to Baby Gaṇeśa who, after feeding at the left breast of his mother, found only a curled-up serpent in place of the right breast. My obeisances to the one in whose dark locks reside the fair Gaṅgā and the crescent moon. Mere thought of you rescues people from the cycle of death and rebirth. You are the source of all knowledge and the inspiration behind the Vedas. Please bless my mother with your beauteous vision."

Whenever the Ācārya sang hymns in praise of a god, his face would flush with excitement. His eyes would close in mystic rapture. As he made up the verses now, his mother was transported with joy, forgetting that she was only moments away from the end. Then there was a brilliant light in the dingy little room which was soon filled with many beings adorned with skulls and tridents and dancing in anticipation of their lord, Śiva. The poor lady was not prepared for this awesome sight. Closing her eyes tightly with both hands, she asked her son to give her a more pleasant vision. The Ācārya then composed a hymn on Viṣṇu who appeared before them flanked by his two consorts and bedecked with gold and diamonds like a blue cloud ringed with lightning. The mother was very pleased with this sight. With peace radiating from her face and thanking her son, she left her mortal body. The Ācārya sat by her side for a few minutes chanting *Om*, tears rolling down his cheeks.

When he sought the help of his relatives to cremate the body, to his surprise he found little sympathy and less assistance forthcoming. Moreover they raised a technical objection. A *sannyāsin* had no right to perform the obsequies of his parents. The *śāstras* as well as tradition forbade it. This upset the Ācārya greatly. He knew the tradition as well as they did, but it was his mother's wish that he should perform her last rites. So he carried the body himself into the cluster of banana trees in the backyard, and made a funeral pyre with dried leaves and bark. He lit the pyre by chanting a mantra invoking Agni, the god of fire. Having thus completed the rites single-handedly, he turned to the village and muttered to himself, more in anguish than in anger, "May this place never have the benefit of a *sannyāsin's* visit. May the brahmins here become ineligible to study the Vedas. And may they all cremate their dead in their own backyards."

Kāladī has yet to recover from this curse.

23
A POOR BOY AND HIS MOTHER

The tales of my Rāmeśvaram pilgrimage inspired not only my friends but also the Ācārya. So, after we had had enough time to rest and after I had recovered completely from the soporific effects of food poisoning, we all set out on a trip to that town. A number of lay people usually joined us on these pilgrimages for the sake of security and company. Some valued the spiritual atmosphere. In our group this time, along with Hastāmalaka, Sureśvara, and Toṭaka, there were King Sudhanvan of Ujjain, and other learned disciples like Samitpāṇi, Cidvilāsa, Jñānakāṇḍa, Viṣṇugupta, Śuddhakīrti, Bhānu Marīci, Kṛṣṇa Darśana, Buddha Viriñci, and Ānanda Giri. There was also an army of attendants to help with various chores. To carry the large library of books and stocks of provisions, we had a caravan of horses and elephants. The attendants would divide themselves into groups, the advance group announcing the arrival of the party to the local rulers or officials by blowing conches and ringing bells. The officials would then meet us on the outskirts of the town or village and make arrangements for our food and lodging.

The Ācārya would address the people and advise them on their problems. These tours were conceived by the Ācārya as a means of emphasizing the unity of the country, north to south and east to west. It meant innumerable hardships for us, but we all felt that we gained from the experience. We valued the firsthand encounters with the life of the country and the problems of the people.

Rāmeśvaram pleased me very much the second time around as I was now in the company of the Ācārya himself.

We visited all the temples. The most famous temple was the one devoted to Lord Śiva's consort. It had one hundred and eight wells inside the compound. We bathed in the water from all of them, an act which was considered meritorious beyond comparison.

After a stay of a week in Rāmeśvaram, our group was fit enough to walk again to the next place, Śrīraṅgam, on the Kāverī , where the renowned temple depicts Viṣṇu as resting on the great serpent Ādiśeṣa. This was the second visit to Śrīraṅgam for some of us, but still the beauty of the temple seemed beyond words. The Ācārya learned that there were at least six different groups of Viṣṇu devotees in this area, each claiming that its own form of worship was the correct one. There were serious misunderstandings and constant quarrels. The Ācārya assembled them all together and explained the unifying principle behind the six narrow approaches. He added that it was important to look for underlying similarities in any array of phenomena and logically minimize the differences. This was sensible because, in matters of faith, there are different ways of reaching the same goal.

When we left Śrīraṅgam for Kāñcī, also for a second visit, we passed through a small village which did not look particularly prosperous. But since it was time for the midday prayers and meal, we stopped there and decided to beg our food in different parts of the village. No one household would be able to feed us all. A few of us were with the Ācārya. We stopped in front of a dilapidated house and the Ācārya, as usual, called aloud, "*Bhavatī, bhikṣāṁ dehi,*" "Mother, please give us alms."

There was no response for a few minutes. As we were

about to move to the next house, the door opened gently and the lady of the house invited us in. She said in great embarrassment, "O Great *Sādhus*, I have heard about you and your tour of the country. I know that there is no greater good in this life than feeding the *sannyāsins* who are the guardians of knowledge and wisdom. Please permit me to give you food this afternoon. I will have it ready by the time you finish your bath. But I must apologize to you in advance for the extreme poverty of the fare. I hope that on that account you will not refuse my hospitality for, if you do, we will be condemned to hell. My husband, who is away at the moment, will not forgive me for transgressing my dharma as a housewife."

She then disappeared into the kitchen and we got busy with our midday routine. In a half hour she announced that food was ready. There was a neat row of banana leaves and we sat in front of them. Slightly away from us, there was another leaf in front of which the lady's five-year old son sat in a sullen mood. The lady served us rice and then the only other item she could scrape for us, a pickle made out of the sour berry, *āmalaka*. Once again she begged that we forgive her inability to provide a better meal. We assured her that it was all right and that we did not want a rich fare, anyway. The little boy however refused to touch his rice. The mother coaxed him to no avail. She was visibly embarrassed for her son's behavior in front of strangers, but did not know what to do.

The Ācārya who had been observing this for some time asked the lady, "Mother, what is the problem? Why does the boy not eat? Is he not well? Does he want something?" She wanted to evade the questions by saying that the boy, lacking in good manners, occasionally became cranky The boy then protested amidst sobs, "Mother, you know I am not a bad boy. You also know that I want my brass plate in which I always eat. Please bring me my plate, won't you, mother?"

In answer to the questioning gaze of the Ācārya, the lady hesitatingly confessed that she had to pawn the boy's plate in order to buy rice for us. She broke down, "I am a wretched woman, indeed. I cannot even feed a few *sādhus* without borrowing money against the little boy's plate. Please forgive me, O God, and at least in the next life provide me the necessary means for hospitality."

These words of utter helplessness brought tears to the Ācārya's eyes, which he closed presently and uttered an anguished prayer to the goddess of wealth. The poem was one of rare beauty as all inspired, unpremeditated poetry is bound to be. "May the grace of the auspicious goddess, who is constantly rejoicing in the company of Viṣṇu, be with me. May the merciful eyes of Lakṣmī be momentarily turned away from her lord so that I can be drenched in the bliss of her divine glance. May the great goddess seated on the thousand-petaled lotus grant me everything that is good. May Śrī Devī, the embodiment of the Vedas, destroy my ignorance and bless me."

The Ācārya then had the vision of the goddess as we could tell from his half-closed eyes filled with tears and trembling lips. He told us later that the goddess asked him a question, "Śaṅkara, even though you prayed that I bless you, I know that you invoked me on behalf of the poor brahmin family. But, tell me, what can I do to help them when they do not have any merit from their past lives to their credit?" The Ācārya, never lacking for a logical response, submitted, "O Merciful Devī, it may be that they did not accumulate any virtue in their previous lives. But the lady has just served us a tasty meal with pickled *āmalaka* going to considerable trouble. Doesn't that count for anything? If you are not convinced, please look at the little boy whose brass plate has been pawned to feed us. Please deign to remove their poverty so that they will never again be in this predicament when guests arrive."

As we were watching the Ācārya in awe, to the surprise of all of us there appeared in front of us a brass plate full of golden *āmalakas.* Our hostess was overcome with joy for now she could feed any number of *sannyāsins* every day. The boy ate happily from his own plate. Thus it is said that even a moment's association with great people brings everlasting bliss and destroys all vestige of sorrow. Shortly afterward we left, anxious to tell about this extraordinary event to our friends elsewhere in the village. The Ācārya himself never spoke about it again, attributing it all to the lady's good fortune.

24

THE PROPER PLACE OF SCHOLARSHIP

A most remarkable feature of the Ācārya's outlook on life was the establishment of goals and priorities. He felt that everything had its place and that one should do different things at different stages of one's life. The supreme goal of a human being is of course Self-realization. One should be able to view things with equanimity. One should be convinced of the equality of all beings regardless of the differences in name and form. The purpose of all learning is to render the student capable of understanding the highest truth through discrimination. Education should civilize a person, not make one arrogant or disdainful of others not equally learned. It is said that learning, wealth, and physical strength are utilized for totally different purposes by good and evil people. The former use them respectively for knowledge, charity, and protection of others, and the latter for disputation, display, and harassment. In matters relating to the spirit, what is important is what you make of your ability and not the ability itself. It was amazing how this mature attitude underlay all activities of one so young.

We all arrived in Kāśī from the south, the Ācārya vanquishing several major and minor philosophical sects en route. This was the second visit there for the Ācārya and me. It was during the first one twelve years ago that I surrendered myself at his holy feet. This time our party stayed there for three months.

One day, as we were walking down the street, the Ācārya noticed on the front porch of a house an old man desperately trying to memorize something. He paused there briefly so he could hear what it was. He thought the old man should not be struggling with whatever it was.

Maybe he could help in some way. So he went closer, and found that the man was committing to memory one of Pāṇini's grammatical rules, *ḍukṛñ karaṇe*. The Ācārya himself was a master of the science of grammar, and he would not have been surprised if the exercise were attempted by a schoolboy. This man had very little time left in this world and he was wasting it on the acquisition of scholastic learning! One became wise only *after* one transcended that phase.

He approached the man and asked him why he was trying to learn grammar at that age. The man, who was having a tough time with his exercise, was annoyed by this interruption. He said as much to the Ācārya, "Pray, sir, what business is it of yours what I do? You have nothing better to do than eat at someone's place and roam the streets. Why don't you leave me alone?" He went back to his grammatical rule with greater gusto.

Sympathizing with the man's utter stupidity, the Ācārya urged him in beautiful verse to become aware of his predicament. "I don't understand your impatience with me. You should know that in you, me, and everyone else, there is the same Viṣṇu. So I suggest that you look upon all alike, seeing yourself in all. Foolish brahmin, spend your time wisely in the service of Viṣṇu as Govinda. Grammatical rules are of no avail when death approaches you.

bhaja govindaṁ bhaja govindaṁ
bhaja govindaṁ, mūḍhamate!
samprāpte sannihite kāle
nahi nahi rakṣati ḍukṛñkaraṇe

"As a child one wastes one's time in play, as a youth in amorous pursuits, and as an old person in futile rumination. Very few, indeed, take the time to think of *Brahman*. While you can, old man, pray to God for the strength to transcend *saṁsāra*, for it is misery to be born and die again and again.

punarapi jananaṁ punarapi maraṇam
punarapi jananījaṭhare śayanam
iha saṁsāre bahudustāre
kṛpayā 'pāre pāhi murāre

"The life of mortals on this planet is unsteady like water on the slippery lotus leaf. It is beset with disease and misery. As long as a man is alive and well, his kinsmen make kind inquiries about him. When he is dead, his own wife is scared of the body.

"Know that wealth brings worry with it; there isn't an iota of happiness in it. The body grows old and infirm with the hair and teeth gone; the man who walks with the aid of a stick still runs after money!

aṅgaṁ galitaṁ palitaṁ muṇḍam
daśanavihīnaṁ jātaṁ tuṇḍam
vṛddho yāti gṛhītvā daṇḍam
tadapi na muñcaty āśāpiṇḍam

"Next to money, the greatest lure for a man in this world is woman. On looking at the bare midriff of a full-breasted woman, don't let desire build up in you. Instead, think of the body as flesh and fat, and blood and bones, which are repelling. Don't pride yourself in your money, relatives, or looks, for all these can be lost in a trice. Know them to be part of a grand illusion. Association with good people leads you to detachment, and detachment frees you from delusion. Then your mind attains steadiness which is the first step toward liberation in this very life.

satsaṅgatve nissaṅgatavam
nissaṅgatve nirmohatvam
nirmohatve niścalatatvā
niścalatatve jīvanmuktiḥ

"One last word: whether you indulge or abstain, if your mind is concentrated on *Brahman*, endless bliss will be yours.

yogarato vā bhogarato vā
saṅgarato vā saṅgavihīnaḥ
yasya brahmaṇi ramate cittam
nandati nandati nandaty eva."

The would-be grammarian saw the point. What was he memorizing Pāṇini for, anyway? What would he do with that knowledge now? It was too late to start a teaching career. Besides, could he really afford to postpone the kind of self-inquiry that the Ācārya was suggesting? Why not try it? He decided to join the Ācārya's group as a lay disciple and learn the other science, the science of the Self.

This little topical poem has since become the instant favorite of the peasant and the scholar throughout the land. Its easy rhymes and rhythms make it fun to repeat and are very appealing to children.

25
WHO NEEDS PHILOSOPHY?

While the Ācārya was writing the commentaries, he would try some of his theories on us. He would incorporate them in his final work only if we all found them acceptable. In these discussions I invariably played the devil's advocate. The Ācārya enjoyed this procedure as much as I did, since it was the best way to give the subject a most logical treatment.

One afternoon I asked the Ācārya a set of particularly tough questions. I knew he could answer them all without any problem but I liked to engage him in debate for the sake of it. It was so delightful to hear him cut through the morass of muddled thinking.

"Sir, you have taught us that Consciousness is unitary and that there is no difference between the subject and the object. But the philosophy of yoga proclaims that *Brahman* and the primordial nature, *Prakṛti*, are two distinct entities. *Brahman* as manifested in man is limited by his nature, and Self-realization consists in removing this limitation in a state of absoluteness. This philosophy also claims that the difference is noted in the scriptures themselves. You say however that the Vedas teach absolute non-dualism. How do you reconcile these two views?"

The Ācārya was obviously pleased with the question. "Padmapāda, it is true that the scriptures talk about a conscious and an unconscious entity as being necessary for creation. The Conscious Being however is the efficient as well as the material cause of creation. Now the point this system of philosophy misses is that the so-called insentient Nature does in fact possess consciousness if only in an *unmanifested* form. The Vedic texts just mean that, because they overwhelmingly speak only of a single consciousness *ultimately*. This I am sure is not hard to believe seeing that a conscious entity like a human being grows hair, nails, etc. which are insentient. The reverse is seen in a situation where worms are born out of a heap of dirt. Thus there is constant traffic between the sentient and insentient entities, which only shows all this is Consciousness, all *Brahman*. There is no room for a separate entity like nature *independent* of *Brahman*.

"However yoga is recommended in the Vedas as a means of Self-realization. So it is useful up to a point, until one learns how to enter the *samādhi* state. There, in its highest form and profoundest experience, there is no seer or the seen. After all, even from the commonsense point of view, the One who created humans, can He not create matter?"

I stated another possible theory of creation. "Suppose that we say that there is no need to posit an intelligent principle for creation at all. In this theory, eternally existing atoms combine and recombine to produce matter. If there is any soul, that too is a material entity. This combination is based on chance, without any coherent principle. What's wrong with that view?"

"Everything. If insentient atoms combine chaotically, who controls their cancerous growth? And what or who prompts them to combine? It is well known that there is no effect without a clearly established cause. What happens when there is the Great Dissolution? Do the atoms disjoin themselves? Again at whose instance, and by what process? More basically, I may ask, what is the difference between a living and a dead body since, in this view, they are both the result of an incoherent union of atoms? You see, there are serious problems."

I had to agree, but then I tried a third approach. "Suppose

we say that, since external things are real, there is no need for individual consciousness."

"All right. How do you know that external things are real?"

"By perception, of course."

"Who perceives?"

"The eye. What else?"

"Does it? Suppose we have a dead body with its eyes open. Do those eyes perceive?

"Well...I suppose not. Let us say then that there is a moment of consciousness on the part of the perceiver. Just long enough for perception to occur."

"Oh, Consciousness is momentary? Does it mean then that, when the eye is not observing the object, the object does not exist? I thought you said that external objects were real."

I had no answer.

"You see, unless you have a constant and unchanging subjective consciousness on the part of the perceiver, no perception takes place. This perceiver is illuminated by consciousness, which is ordinarily veiled by nescience because the perceiver superimposes limitations such as the body and mind upon it. It is this superimposition that is responsible for false perception, not the momentariness of consciousness. Once the veil is removed, that is when the consciousness is in an unmodified and uncircumscribed state, there is only itself and neither the perceiver nor the perceived because they are both unreal."

"Let us consider God as the efficient cause of the universe, in which case He becomes the overseer of the affairs of the world."

"In that view I you would say that God, soul,

and Nature are eternally distinct."

"Even so."

"Then what would you say is the relationship between Him and the creation?"

"That of master and servant."

"Then how does the master handle the affairs of the servant? That is, based on what principle? As he pleases? He would subject Himself to charges of arbitrariness, injustice, etc."

"Suppose the governing principle is that of karma as in non-dualism."

"Even then it doesn't work because why should God manage others' affairs in which he is interested? Therefore He must have a *selfish* interest which is unthinkable."

I fired one last shot.

"Let me take the position then that individual souls are the *products* of God and share in His Consciousness."

"So what? Once the individual self is *born*, regardless of the source, it is liable to be impermanent, like any other originated entity. Also the question arises as to the relative importance of God and His product. Are they different? If they are, as you said, the one who is born is bound to die. If they are equal in all respects, then either one will do; there is no need for both. Now, are there any other theories you want to put forth?"

Of course I had none. But whatever had been discussed so far was immensely pleasing to me and my friends. Our faith in the logical and pragmatic excellence of non-dualism was more firmly established than ever.

I wondered however about someone who might say, "Why should I care about any philosophy at all? I am doing fine the way I am. I have no problems."

"If this person is really contented, that's fine. He is probably a realized soul. But if he is an ordinary person too lazy to think and face reality, then he is wasting his life. He is just being an animal or a vegetable."

The Ācārya's answer seemed to apply to the vast majority of the people and the way they led their lives.

NĪLAKAṆṬHA, THE ŚAIVAITE

Our party was traveling down the west coast. The sea looked muddy and noisy. The Ācārya stared at it in silent contemplation. The waves looked as though swarms of petty controversialists were advancing toward the all-knowing and all-vanquishing Ācārya and receding on meeting with stern rebuffs.

We reached Gokarṇam. Having bathed in the sea, the Ācārya worshipped Lord Śiva in the temple. In the afternoon, he addressed the local residents who had come to pay him their respects. He told them how to cope with life's ups and downs and how they should set aside a short period of time during the day for meditation and self-inquiry. One should surrender to the Lord if one could. If one had the reasoning ability, one could see the illusoriness of the world. Then nothing would matter; it would all appear to be a grand show by the Creator, perhaps for His own amusement. On these occasions, the Ācārya rarely mentioned such advanced concepts as *advaita* and the identity of individual and universal souls. A good teacher knows his class.

Just then one of the younger disciples who went into the village returned very excited. As soon as he got the Ācārya's attention, he gushed, "Sir, I am sorry to interrupt but this is too much. As your pupils, we feel it's an insult to us."

The Ācārya calmed him down and asked, "What is the matter, my child? What's too much? Who insulted you, and why?"

Somewhat composed by now, the young pupil explained. "Sir, I was walking down the main street a short while ago. As I passed by a large house, I saw a Śaiva scholar surrounded by a handful of disciples. One of them pointed to me and said, 'There goes a pupil of the new Ācārya who is camping in our village. Ācārya Śaṅkara is said to have defeated all the scholars in the north, east, and south. He is considered omniscient and invincible in debate.' These remarks elicited a sneer from the scholar--I believe his name is Nīlakaṇṭha--who said aloud, 'My boy, what are you talking about? You know that I, Nīlakaṇṭha, have written a great commentary on the *Brahmasūtra* along the lines of the Śaiva doctrine. Everyone around here is scared to lock horns with me in philosophical combat. And you say that this Saṅkara, whose name I haven't even heard, is considered superior to me? Know that he can't even equal me, let alone excel. You will now see for yourself how the brilliance of my dialectics will shatter the ignorance of this self-styled Ācārya.'"

The boy paused for breath and then continued. "O Great Sir, I ran here to convey this news to you. Nīlakaṇṭha and his group are close by. Please beat this man in argument and put him in his place for our sake, even if you are not interested yourself."

The Ācārya asked the youth to relax. "All right, I shall debate with Nīlakaṇṭha--for your sake. Don't worry."

Nīlakaṇṭha's party had arrived by now. More than his followers, Nīlakaṇṭha himself was in a belligerent mood. Seeing the man's poor manners, my friend Sureśvara came up to the Ācārya and said, "Sir, leave this pompous ass of a pundit to me. You need not waste your time on him." But before the Ācārya could respond, Nīlakaṇṭha turned to the Ācārya and shouted, "I want to debate with you, not any of your students. I consider you my adversary. If you are not prepared, you'd better admit defeat."

Upon the Ācārya consenting to debate, Nīlakaṇṭha started his attack. "What the *advaita* says about the individual soul and the Creator being identical is ridiculous. The analogy with the sun and its reflection in glass and water does not hold good because the Creator and the creature are distinct entities. But any onlooker can, on the other hand, see both the sun and the reflection and certify their identity. There is no point in saying that the cow and horse are the same animal, once you eliminate their 'cowness' and 'horseness.' The difference between two independent entities can never be sublated."

The Ācārya was not in the least perturbed by this onslaught on non-duality. He had heard these arguments before and had adequately dealt with them in his commentary. He quietly began. "Learned Śaiva, you have made your point. Now, listen. In the Upaniṣadic declaration *tat tvam asi,* 'That you are,' it is true that there is a formal difference between 'That' and 'you,' just as there is a difference between 'he' and 'man' in the sentence 'He is a man.' But the difference is only in the direct meaning of the words concerned, not in the implied meaning which establishes the identity of 'he' and 'man.' It is Pure Consciousness that is indicated by both *tat* and *tvam.* Now *tat* is the Creator and *tvam* is the embodied second person. Thus, even though the Creator and a human being in flesh and blood are superficially unequatable, in terms of consciousness that underlies both of them, they are identical. In the case of the cow and the horse you referred to, there is no such substratum of pure awareness, though they, too, share some degree of consciousness. So their similarity is of a lower degree. In the ultimate analysis all creation is permeated by consciousness, the degree of permeation varying from one entity to another. In man alone consciousness resides in a pure form even though only few realize it."

Nīlakaṇṭha persisted. "How can you say that two different bodies which experience separate joys and sorrows are one and the same? We see the duality as a matter of daily occurrence. The difference in the experience of, say, a king and a beggar would be unexplainable in your theory. The only way to explain duality of experience is to posit duality of agency. Two different agents, two different experiences. It's as simple as that. You might also wish to consider the nature of liberation which, according to you, is a state of bliss. But we dualists say that it is an elimination of sorrow. If it were merely happiness, there is always the threat of sorrow which, in nature, goes hand in hand with happiness."

The Ācārya now gave the definitive answer. "Dual experiences like happiness and misery, and cold and heat, are merely your mental constructs. They do not affect the soul, the *ātman* of the human being, and have therefore no basis in reality. They exist only in the different adjuncts of the *ātman* such as a king's body, a beggar's body, a thief's body, etc. The sense of agency is also based on this adjunct, because Pure Consciousness cannot have either subjectivity or objectivity. The happiness and sorrow you speak of are born out of sensory apprehension. The *advaitin's* happiness is bliss, the bliss of the very existence. It is neither dependent on any external circumstance nor is it affected by any."

Neither Nīlakaṇṭha's dialectics nor his theology was a match for the Ācārya's logical presentation of the Truth, backed by his firsthand experience. Being a learned scholar, Nīlakaṇṭha was able to appreciate the strength of the Ācārya's position.

My young friend, who started it all, was the happiest of all.

27

MISCONCEPTIONS ABOUT REALITY

I noticed that, while sometimes the dualists and others wanted to engage the Ācārya in debate, at other times the Ācārya himself wanted to tackle certain well-known scholars of non-monistic persuasions. In fact this was one of the reasons that sometimes prompted his visit to a certain place.

We were now in the famous city of Ujjain on the banks of the Śiprā. Lord Śiva manifested himself there as Mahākāla. The Ācārya rested there for a bit, and then told me, "Padmapāda, in the city there is a scholar of great repute by name Bhaṭṭa Bhāskara. He is very well-read and has a large following. He is in fact the last among the great scholars that I have to help realize the Truth. Go seek him and tell him that I am in town. He can see me at his convenience."

I was surprised to hear about this new scholar whom the Ācārya regarded so highly. I was at the same time sure that no one could come anywhere near the Ācārya's attainments. So the message got slightly altered in the delivery. "I am Padmapāda, a disciple of the world's greatest teacher, Ācārya Śaṅkara. I presume you have heard of him. He has defeated in argumentation various scholars of schools opposed to non-dualism. In his great commentary on the *Brahmasūtra*, he has refuted all dualistic doctrines including yours and made them look ridiculously untenable. He now wishes to meet you in person, that is, if you don't give up your false thinking and surrender at his feet."

Bhāskara was understandably annoyed with my message and the tone in which it was delivered. "You say that your Ācārya refuted my doctrines? Perhaps he doesn't know that I move among my opponents like a swan among lotus stalks, and I gobble them up. I faulted even ancient teachers like Kapila and Kaṇāda. Your teacher doesn't have a chance. I will prove he is a mere dwarf before this giant of a scholar."

"O Great Bhaṭṭa, you may have been a swan among the lotus stalks. But you will find my Ācārya to be the mighty hawk, Garuḍa, the transport of Viṣṇu Himself. You may have been a chisel to the rocky slopes of opposing philosophies but you will find the Ācārya to be Mount Meru which is as hard as a diamond. But why all this talk? I suggest you prepare yourself for a resounding defeat at the hands of the Ācārya."

I returned to the Ācārya. The Bhaṭṭa arrived close on my heels. The Ācārya stood up and cordially invited him in, much to my embarrassment. The Bhaṭṭa also was somewhat mollified by now in unspoken acknowledgment of the Ācārya's personal magnetism. He was not however prepared to acknowledge the supremacy of *advaita*. So he went right at it.

"O *Sannyāsin*, your position is that illusion or *māyā* is responsible for the differentiation between the individual and the Lord? Then where does *māyā* come from? It must emanate from either the one or the other—in which case, the distinction is automatically implied. Right?"

"No. Māyā rests on Pure Consciousness, and not on either the Creator or the individual. Just like the image of an object in a mirror. The object precedes the image. Māyā is just an image of Pure Consciousness. Both the Creator and the individual are characterized by this adjunct of Pure Consciousness, but they temporarily become unaware of their connection with it. Hence the apparent difference between the Creator and the human being, who are merely playing different roles in the cosmic drama. How can they, having originated from the same source, ever be different in reality?"

"How can *māyā*, something unconscious in itself, be located in Pure Consciousness?" queried Bhāskara. "It must be found only in the individual who sometimes says 'I am ignorant.'"

"No, we cannot conclude that way, because the individual can also say, 'I am a self-conscious being.'"

"*Māyā* depends upon one's mind which is made of inert matter, and hence creates the feeling of ignorance in a human being."

"But the mind itself is a product of *māyā*, as they are both insentient. Besides, in dreamless sleep, the mind does not function. But *māyā* is always present."

"I disagree. *Māyā* is also absent in deep sleep, according to the scriptures."

According to the scripture, *māyā* *is* present. The text says that in deep sleep one is not aware of it. In order for one to be aware of something, it must exist."

"If *māyā* has its locus in Pure Consciousness, then is it a temporary or permanent condition? I don't think it is permanent because consciousness and unconsciousness cannot coexist. If it is temporary, then how is it removed from Pure Consciousness? Or is it irremovable? We know it is not irremovable because a state of pure knowledge is possible to those who realize *Brahman.* The conclusion therefore is that ignorance is neither permanent nor temporary and cannot be associated with awareness at all. Then the question that I have to answer is, How is the world apprehended?' and the answer is 'through illusory perception.'"

The Ācārya countered, "What is this 'illusory perception?"

"'I am a man' is an illusion. 'I am *Brahman*' is valid knowledge."

"That's not what your identity-in-difference theory suggests. For you all perceptions are real, since both identity and difference are constantly present in all entities."

The Bhaṭṭa plodded on. "No, this is not true. When a perception is known to be right, a preceding perception is given up as illusory. When it is perceived that 'I am *Brahman*' is correct, the perception 'I am man' disappears."

The Ācārya smiled. "Now, wait a minute. If both identity and difference are constantly present, then two perceptions of the individual as a human being and as *Brahman* must be real. You are unintentionally crossing over to our system of thinking when you say that a later, valid perception negates the earlier, incorrect perception."

"This is not a universal fact, because identity-in-difference is posited only in respect of certain pairs such as part and whole, cause and effect, etc."

"All right. Let's take the part-whole relation. According to this, the body and the spirit should both be real. Then the feeling 'I am the body' will never go."

The Bhaṭṭa then asked earnestly. "How do you

overcome this great *māyā* which is rooted in Awareness itself?"

The Ācārya replied, dispelling his doubts once and for all. "It is not right to say that *māyā* is *rooted* in consciousness. It is but a reflection thereof. It can be eliminated through knowledge and meditation on the unmodified mental state such as one obtains in deep sleep. Only the consciousness is real. *Māyā* is unreal, though it is projected by the same consciousness. Therefore the statement 'I am *Brahman*' is valid, 'I am a human being' is not, because it has ignorance for its basis."

The Bhaṭṭa realized the problem with his dualistic perception of life and his identity-in-difference approach. He decided to become a disciple of the Ācārya, destroying his own commentarial work.

* * * * * *

In the assemblage of people that had gathered to witness the learned disputations of the Ācārya and the Bhaṭṭa, there was a Jaina who thought he had all the answers to the Ācā rya's questions. He challenged the Ācārya.

"Why don't you accept the seven-fold Jaina view of reality in terms of the soul, inanimate objects, sensuous attraction, control of the senses, austerity, bondage, and liberation?"

The Ācārya's patience was monumental. A lot of times when he could directly tear down the opponent's argument, he still engaged in discussion until the opponent himself discovered his error. In the present case, he readily admitted that Vardhamāna, the founding father of Jainism, was a great sage even as Siddhārtha was. The trouble lay only with the perversity of imperfect understanding by his followers of the reasoning behind the preceptor's methods.

The Ācārya asked the Jaina, "What is the nature of the individual soul in your doctrine?"

"The individual soul is exactly the same size as the body that it occupies. It is controlled by eight types of karma—"

"Never mind the karma. You say the soul's size is the same as the body it inhabits. That is, an elephant has a vastly bigger soul than does a mosquito. And, as the body grows bigger, the soul grows. When it shrinks, the soul also shrinks, right?"

"Right."

"In that case, what you are talking about is the non-self, and not the Self. A soul by definition is unchanging and imperishable. Anything that expands and contracts will also die. So it cannot be the *ātman*. Now did you say that the soul is sentient or insentient?"

"The soul is sentient. And when there is a large body that needs to be tenanted, more than one soul gets in."

"Doesn't it appear strange to you that several sentient souls can at once dwell in the same body? Won't they pull in several different directions then?"

"No, they won't. It's just like a chariot pulled by many horses, all going in the same direction."

"Ah, but you are forgetting the charioteer, who coordinates their movement. Who coordinates the many-souled body?"

The Jaina did not know. Now, why did he not think of that before?

Further on in the west, at Dvārakā, the native town of Śrī Kṛṣṇa, there were famed and ferocious Vaiṣṇava polemicists who wore *tulasī* leaves behind their ears to signify their religious affiliation. Them, too, the Ācārya defeated. The main flaw in their arguments which were generally closely based on the Vedas, was that they claimed for their souls individual status even when they attained the world of Viṣṇu. They argued that otherwise they would not be able to enjoy the fruits of all their devotions. The Ācārya pointed out the puerility of this justification, asking them why they would want to stop just short of total bliss. If they had in mind the pleasures of heaven and the world of gods, then their realization was not complete. As long as there was the slightest differentiation between *Brahman* and the individual, there was no liberation.

28
THE ĀCĀRYA, A VICTIM OF BLACK MAGIC

The Ācārya now in Kāmarūpa in the far eastern section of the country. The town was famous for the temple of *Śakti* as Kāmākhyā. It was also well known for its small but powerful band of tantrics called Śāktas noted for their superstition and barbarity.

The leader of the Śāktas, Navagupta, wanted to eliminate the Ācārya who defeated him in debate. He knew that there was no other way of stopping the imminent demise of his cult, just like the Kāpālika before in Śrī Śailam. He thought he would use his ample occult powers to achieve his end. And there was just the recipe in his book of magic formulas. Using the *abhicārī* form of black magic, he was able to produce in the Ācārya a most painful and incurable anal fistula.

The disease grew in the Ācārya's body with uncanny rapidity. While he did not say a word about it to anybody, we soon noticed that he was losing weight and was eating less and less. While washing his clothes, Toṭaka saw blood stains on them. We became worried about this dreadful ailment but did not know what to do about it. The only thing we could think of was to petition the Ācārya himself.

"Revered Ācārya, perhaps you haven't noticed it but your body is getting weaker by the day. All your disciples are very worried about it. There must be a serious disorder that is gnawing at your vitals and we pray that you do something about it. Even if you do not care about your body, as your disciples we ought to do all that is in our power to restore your health. There are many distinguished physicians in the country who can diagnose and cure the most intractable of maladies in no time. Please permit us to call them in, and please allow yourself to be treated. You are our only support and we cannot be without the sight of your divine form even for one minute."

As we expected, the Ācārya was not worried about his health at all. "Diseases are the result of past karma and will disappear as soon as the karma is exhausted. There is no need to worry about them. And there is no use worrying, because they take their own course, anyway. Therefore I do not believe that any treatment by physicians is necessary. If the body withers and drops in the meantime, so be it. It does not bother me in the least."

"It is true, Sir, that you are not in the least interested in the continuance of the physical frame. But you must accept medicine for our sake. It is not just us, the entire world depends on you."

The Ācārya did not respond. We took his silence for acquiescence and, after considerable searching, located a couple of competent physicians in the court of the neighboring prince. They made sure they received a fat fee first, for which we had to beg a local merchant. They examined the Ācārya, nodded their heads in thoughtful consultation, and applied remedies as best they could. To their utter embarrassment nothing seemed to work.

After many days of futile effort on the part of the good doctors, the Ācārya told them, "It is said in our tradition that to the patient the medicine is like the curative water from the holy Gaṅgā and the physician Viṣṇu Himself. But in my case, because of my strong karma, your salves have been to no avail. Do not feel bad. It is no reflection on your competence. You have been away from your families too long. They will be eagerly awaiting your return home. Moreover, your employer, the king, has been without the benefit of your services all these days. So you must go back and make them all happy. As for me, it seems I will have to endure my affliction for some more time." The doctors, now devoid of some of their professional arrogance and feeling bad for receiving the fee without really earning it, left reluctantly.

More days passed, but still there was no improvement in the Ācārya's condition. In fact, it worsened visibly. Out of curiosity and at the instance of all of us, the Ācārya agreed to find out and tell us the cause of his disease. He then sat in meditation in a quiet corner of the temple compound. In about half an hour, he came back smiling and said that what caused his disease was Navagupta's black magic for which there was no cure.

No sooner did I hear this from the lips of the unperturbed Ācārya, then my blood began to course through my veins. Heat was emanating from every pore of my body. I felt like destroying the whole blasted tribe of the lowly, miserable Śāktas without a trace. How dare these wretches do this to my Ācārya? These rascals should not be allowed to tread Mother Earth. Then I wondered how best to handle the situation and save the Ācārya from the treachery of the vicious Navagupta. I could once again invoke the power of the terrible man-lion, Narasiṁha, and make short work of the diabolical Navagupta, but that would be too easy on him. What I had in mind for him was different. He should suffer at least ten times as long as the Ācārya had and die writhing in agony at the end. But the Ācārya must not know any of this for, if he did, he would surely prohibit it. So in the middle of the night, I moved a little distance away from where everyone was sleeping and chanted the supreme mantra *Om* for an hour with the specific objective of destroying Navagupta. The same primal syllable, repeated without any specific object in mind, would grant enlightenment and spiritual solace. The whole science of sound is beyond the comprehension of ordinary mortals. The fistula was then transferred immediately to the evil Śākta to the same spot as on the Ācārya's body.

That was the end of Navagupta, the black magician.

29
THE THRONE OF OMNISCIENCE

Not long after his recovery from Navagupta's black magic, the Ācārya was sitting on the dry river bed in quiet meditation. He withdrew his senses and attained a state of consciousness in which he was one with all creation. He was experiencing the Truth that he had been preaching. The Truth was what he formally learnt from his teacher Govindapāda. The Truth was what he had studied and commented upon in Gauḍapāda's exposition of the *Māṇḍūkya Upaniṣad*. As he was meditating on the contribution of the great Gauḍapāda, the sage himself appeared in his vision and addressed him.

"Saṅkara, my disciple Govinda imparted the supreme knowledge of the *ātman* to you and you have put it to good use by exposing the defects of all other doctrines. I am very pleased with you." The Ācārya was overwhelmed by the great guru's kindness. "Revered Sir, whatever accomplishments I have are entirely due to your grace and that of my guru. To one who has received the guru's kindness nothing is impossible. The mute can become eloquent, the lame can scale the mountain, and a fool can become a Vedic scholar in no time. I am indeed fortunate to see you who are an embodiment of Pure Awareness."

"Dear child, my student Govinda told me all about the great commentary you wrote on my work. I would like to know more about how you dealt with it. Though I am beyond all attachments, your company gives me much happiness." The Ācārya then bowed to him in humility and read out his work. Gauḍapāda was immensely pleased with his commentary and how he interpreted his work exactly as he would have done himself. He offered a boon to the Ācārya as an expression of his pleasure, but the Ācārya politely declined saying, "O Sage of Sages, you have already conferred on me the greatest boon--that of your grace. That's more than I deserve." Gauḍapāda then blessed him and disappeared from his consciousness. The Ācārya was very excited as he narrated these details to us in the evening.

* * * * * * *

The next morning we all assembled in the presence of the Ācārya and were talking about all the famous places of learning in the country. Some said the best place was Kāśī, others said it was Kāñcī, yet others Kāshmīr, and Takṣaśilā. In the discussion it came out that there was a place close to Śrīnagar in Kāshmīr famed as Śāradā Pīṭha, the seat of the goddess of learning. In that place there was a temple dedicated to Śāradā with entrances on all four sides. The main entrance on each side led through a series of inner doorways to the central hall large enough to accommodate thousands of people. In the center of the hall, there was a throne made of exquisite marble inlaid with diamonds and sapphires which lit the hall with their brilliance. This throne was called the throne of omniscience because only a person who knows all the branches of learning without exception was allowed to sit on it. Being allowed to occupy the throne was the highest honor in the land. Only a handful of scholars ever claimed the right to ascend it and fewer still were accepted after being tested by the scores of pundits in residence. Depending on the part of the country to which an aspirant belonged, he attempted to enter from the south, west, north, or the east gate.

It so happened that until then there had been no scholar from the south at all to claim the throne. It seemed to us that the Ācārya's omniscience should be proclaimed to the world. We prayed to him in unison. "Sir, we all feel that you should ascend the throne of omniscience entering the temple from the southern gate. This accomplishes two things: the world will know that you are all-knowing, and that the south, too, produced an all-knowing person. Then your winning the right to the throne is the same as *advaita* being granted recognition as the Supreme Truth. Please do not deny our request."

The Ācārya had heard of the throne of omniscience but never considered claiming it. Being a great debater himself, he realized the futility of all debate in the ultimate analysis when one dealt with one's own soul. Besides he had already stilled many discordant religious voices in the country and clearly established the Vedic dharma. There was no need for him to prove that he was personally all-knowing. That did not matter at all. But we all finally prevailed upon him, and our group started toward Kāshmīr a few days later.

As our party reached Śāradā temple, our attendants began to shout. "Hail to the Ācārya! Hail to the Ācārya who has muted all opponents in argument! Make way for the lion among *advaitins* who has smashed the foreheads of dualist elephants and struck terror into the hearts of all controversialists! Make way for the illustrious Ācārya who intends to ascend the throne of omniscience!" When the Ācārya reached the southern gate and attempted to enter, a dozen pundits barred his way and declared, "You seeker of fame, don't be in a hurry to enter. You must prove that you are omniscient before you can do so." The Ācārya said that he would abide by their regulations and answer the questions put by the various specialists among them.

The first scholar to question the Ācārya was a follower of the philosophy of atomism as set forth by Kaṇāda. "Two atoms, in our view, fuse together to form a single subtle particle. If, as you claim, you are omniscient, tell me what is responsible for such fusion."

The Ācārya readily responded. "It is the inherent property of the two atoms that makes them fuse into a unit." This was the right answer.

Then a vainglorious scholar of logic sauntered forth at the next doorway and asked the Ācārya, "If your claim to omniscience is not a bluff, tell me in what way Gautama's school of logic differs from Kaṇāda's in respect of the concept of *mokṣa*"

"In Kaṇāda's view, liberation is a state free of all qualities; it is like space. Gautama makes it also blissful and sentient. Both accept God as the Creator of this universe, but in the enumeration of categories Kaṇāda has seven and Gautama sixteen." The logician was satisfied.

The next doorway was guarded by a Sāṁkhya man who lay in wait for the Ācārya. "Is nature dependent or independent of an intelligent being?" This was an old question for the Ācārya. "*Prakṛti*, characterized by three qualities and forming the universe, is independent of an intelligent being in Sāṁkhya. But we say it is dependent on a Creator."

Then the Buddhists asked, "What is the difference between our idealist theory and your philosophy?"

"The idealists look upon consciousness as momentary; it is a series of fleeting impressions. We say it is permanent, imperishable, and unitary."

The Buddhists had a further question. "What is the difference between the two kinds of Realism?"

"According to one of your schools, reason alone is responsible for the apprehension of things. According to the other, perception is the principal means of ascertaining the truth."

Next it was the Jaina's turn. This one belonged to the *au naturel* sect. "What is meant by *astikāya* in our system?"

"The Jainas refer to five *astikāyas* or categories, namely those of the body, merit, demerit, space, and soul." The Jaina was surprised at the Ācārya's detailed knowledge of his faith.

The last one to query the Ācārya was a follower of Jaimini's ritualist school. "Is sound a substance or quality?"

"Sound is the form of the Eternal Letter, and is an all-pervading substance in your school." Looking about him with a smile, the Ācārya asked suavely, "Any more questions?" He saw no one coming forward. Then holding my hand the Ācārya walked up to the throne. As he was about to be seated on it, there was divine music coming from the image of Śāradā behind the throne followed by a voice, "Śaṅkara, you have proven to the satisfaction of all that you are learned in all the *śāstras* and systems of philosophy. However, there is an important requirement that one who aspires for this seat of learning must fulfill. He must have led an absolutely pure life. You spent some time in the company of women while in the body of King Amaruka. Do you think that you fulfill that requirement satisfactorily?"

The Ācārya knew this was the voice of the goddess herself. He had an answer to her question, too. "Mother Śāradā, what I did in another physical form does not in the least affect the purity of this body with which I am about to occupy this celebrated seat. This body has not committed any transgressions since its birth. So I fulfill your requirement without a doubt." The voice then became silent, having accepted the explanation. The Ācārya thereupon sat on the throne of omniscience. There was much hilarity and joy among us disciples and spectators as flowers rained from above. According to the poet, the celestial maidens had to go without floral decorations in their coiffures for many days afterwards.

30

A FEW URGENT QUESTIONS ANSWERED

The Ācārya announced today that we could have a question-answer session. We could ask any question we liked, theoretical or practical. The junior disciples sort of looked up to me, though Sureśvara was much older. So I asked the first question.

"Revered Sir, you said earlier that one way of gaining *Brahman* knowledge is to inquire who we are. But when I do that, the answer that I get is that I am Padmapāda, son of so-and-so and disciple of the great Ācārya Śaṅkara. Further, I know that I am learned in the Vedas and *śāstras* and perhaps have a few other abilities. In what way does such an inquiry help me?" Even though we had gone over this topic dozens of times, I asked the question once again for the benefit of the others in the group who were not too sure of the answer.

"Padmapāda, though some of you already know the answer, that's a good question to begin our discussion with. The 'I' that you are talking about is not the Self but the ego associated with the mind and the senses. It gives the feeling 'I am the doer.' It produces not absolute but relative knowledge of subject and object. The knowledge vanishes when the ego is absent in deep sleep."

"So how should we inquire, Sir?"

"As you keep on inquiring who this superficial 'I' is and where it comes from, you will realize that the real 'I', the Self, is beyond action, intellect, ratiocination, etc. and is the substratum of those and other possible mental states. Further inquiry along these lines makes clear that the phenomenal world is relative and exists only when you are awake. But your Self, the consciousness, is ever present."

"Then this self-inquiry seems to be a simpler method of attaining liberation than the other techniques we have studied. Is that correct?"

"Yes, in a way. People practice austerities, devotion, ritual, as well as self-inquiry to achieve liberation. Self-inquiry is perhaps a direct, commonsense approach. One thing to remember, though, is that liberation is not some kind of new status to be gained. It is already there. You just have to experience it. When the ego starts receding into the background as a result of self-inquiry, realization starts coming in your line of vision. Reality is the absence of ego."

"How do I know that the Self is not the body?"

"Is there a self in the dead body?" The Ācārya countered.

Some of the junior students now got into the act and started asking several vaguely related questions.

"Sir, kindly tell us about death."

"Death is an insignificant physical event like birth. Strictly speaking, one is neither born nor is ever dead because birth and death are within the realm of the ego which is attached to the body. One who is evolved is indifferent to both phenomena. Fear of death is due to one's identification with the body. People keep thinking of someone as a body and so that someone is either born or dead. But if you suspend the ordinary thought process, that body and, in fact, all bodies, cease to exist. The real you is eternal, without birth or death. So get rid of the false 'I'."

"What happens at death?"

"Speech recedes into the mind; the mind disappears into the breath; the breath then seeks refuge in the Lord, that is, Self. This Self is individualized when enveloped by karma and the attributes of the ten organs, mind, and intellect, and travels forth in quest of a new body in accordance with the inexorable law of karma."

"What happens *after* death? How long after one's death is one reborn?"

"Why do you want to know? All this knowledge is only as real as the ego. It doesn't alter the basic Truth. Depending on the karma a body has to work off, some are reborn almost immediately and others after some time. Some are reborn on this planet but will eventually attain liberation on some higher plane. Very few souls are liberated here and now."

"O Ācārya, since death is not to be feared at all, there is no fear at all in this world?"

"Right. There is no fear. Now, think. Fear arises only because of a second person, one other than yourself. When there is no other person, where's the fear? Fear is another trick of the mind. The Self knows no fear. Similarly, there is no grief, no pain, because they, too, are notions associated with the mind which is an instrument of the ego."

"Does it mean then that if someone hurts me I feel no pain?"

"That is correct, if you succeed in separating your Self from your body. When you withdraw the illumination of the Self or consciousness from the brain and its mechanism, you have effectively destroyed all sensation including pain. Such a withdrawal is possible through yoga or meditation. On a small scale, we all routinely accomplish this feat when we say 'I don't know when I got hurt but I see the scratch now."

" Sir, does it mean then that pleasure is unreal?"

"Of course, it does. It is only because of the association of your mind that you realize that something is pleasant. Just shut off your mind once and then try to experience what is usually considered pleasant. It is just not possible. This applies to all physical or sense pleasures including sex. A woman's breasts are so much fat and tissue and don't mean anything by themselves. It is when the touch is associated with a certain mental conditioning that pleasurable feelings are aroused. In other words, every time there is a pleasant or unpleasant object presented to your ego, it tells you that you should enjoy it or avoid it. Suppose you pause to look at the stimulus as it really is, then you remain totally unaffected. You don't have to be a philosopher or an ascetic to realize this."

"How do we know that there are past lives?"

"It is an unexceptionable physical and psychological principle that whatever you do produces a related effect. At death, the soul, i.e. the individual self, carries with it myriad subtle impressions and these impressions then determine in the next life whether a person will turn to be a saint or a villain, a scholar or a fool. Nothing is ever erased from cosmic memory. We can't explain the difference among the people that we see in any other way. We say that some are 'gifted.' Where does the child get this gift from? Even the sage can at best hope to transcend the effects of karma by means of his knowledge, but he must suffer through them, too. No one can escape it altogether."

"Does one have to renounce one's family to realize *Brahman*?"

"Certainly not. Detachment is necessarily more difficult

in the case of a householder but he is as qualified to perform the above self-inquiry as the ascetic. What matters is what you do with your mind. There is the story of two friends, one a pious brahmin who went to the temple everyday, and the other a rake who visited a prostitute equally regularly. However the rake always thought of his friend in the temple, while the brahmin thought of the prostitute and the good time his friend was having. When they died, the brahmin went to hell and the lecher to heaven. The mind therefore does play tricks on you and you have got to use it very carefully. You do need it initially, but like the stick used to poke the funeral pyre, it should be destroyed in the end to realize the Self."

"What is the role of ascetics in the society, Sir? Aren't they a burden?"

"Certainly not. For one thing their needs are few. For another, their instruction to the community is a sobering influence and leads people along the path of virtue. Their very presence is a boon to troubled minds."

"Sir, is it true that a yogi achieves great miracles and attains many *siddhis*?"

"Yes, it is true. The ability to perform miracles can be acquired through birth, drugs, magic, or meditation. But the seeker after Truth spurns them because they push him down the depths of ego. Incidentally, those who perform miracles do no claim that they are performing miracles. To them they are natural, following different natural laws from the ordinary ones. All matter obeys one who has mastered his mind. But the real ascetic has no use for them."

"What is the effect of drugs on a person? Why can't we take them to produce miracles?"

"As I told you, miracles are to be shunned because they

are the products of the ego and are impediments to self-realization. Drugs have the effect of disorienting your thinking and veiling your consciousness even more than it ordinarily is. Why drown what little surface consciousness you have in a narcotic stupor?"

Then a young disciple who joined us newly hesitatingly addressed the Ācārya. "Illustrious Sir, may I ask about something that has been bothering me for some time?"

"Surely, my child. There is nothing to hide here. We are all trying to understand the reasons for our ignorance and find out the means to cast it off."

"How can we get rid of the sex urge, which is the strongest of all physical urges? Food, sex, and sleep are said to be the distinguishing characteristics of all animals including humans."

"As we have been saying all along, any desire arises owing to the feeling of difference between the subject and the object, which are in fact manifestations of the same Self. The Self has no sex and no second. When there is no second person, there is no urge. Moreover, you must never identify yourself with your body. You love others for the sake of the Self."

"If all this world is Self, one universal consciousness, why was it created at all with such diversity?"

"This is for the sport of the Self, just as we entertain ourselves with various sports, even though they have no apparent purpose."

"Revered Ācārya, you said a while back that meditation is one of the ways to realize one's selfhood. Can you kindly tell us a little bit more about meditation?"

"Meditation is, strictly speaking, being established in

unitary consciousness but, in common parlance, it has come to mean the effort required for this purpose. You experience this unitary consciousness in deep sleep every day based on the fact that you don't know what happens then. In other words, your consciousness then is unmodified, unfragmented. Such a state can be voluntarily achieved in *samādhi*, the yogic trance in which only consciousness remains in its pristine purity."

I asked one last question before the session concluded. "How do we know that we are not deluding ourselves into thinking that there is a super-consciousness which controls our destinies and that its realization is our ultimate goal?"

The Ācārya's smile was tolerant. "How do you know that you are not deluding yourself when you think that the world is real along with its trials and tribulations? What's delusion?" Your being a self? Your possessing senses which are defunct in deep sleep thereby annulling the world for you? Or your possession of a consciousness which is shared by all the universe? Is it then difficult to see that this unitary consciousness is our real nature in its pure form? You often speak of a conscience which is occasionally in conflict with your actions and desires. What is this conscience? Is it also not common knowledge, both from authentic stories of reincarnation and direct evidence of supernormal phenomena, that there is a hidden dimension to our existence? It is this dimension that our sages and seers explored to the fullest in the Vedas and related revelations and passed on the results to us. That is why we say that the Vedas are authoritative, being records of experiments in spirit. They testify to the immense potential in all of us. You cannot say, my dear Padmapāda, that the world's mystics and saints were all deluded."

"I am sorry, Sir, if my question seemed impertinent. I wanted to strengthen my own conviction regarding the realm of the spirit by your unequivocal instruction. As a matter of fact, from my own limited experience, I know that one enhances one's own *ātmic* power as one progresses in one's practices from contemplation to concentration to *samādhi*. Further, I also thought that some of my younger friends here might be benefited from a well-deserved condemnation of the materialism of the type advocated by Cārvāka and his misled followers."

"Dear Padmapāda, you have rightly referred to the school of Cārvāka as misguided. It's not very difficult to see its folly. All that Cārvāka wanted was a nice and easy life for himself with no work. It was a childish, selfish, and impractical philosophy. The trouble with hedonism is that it just does not work even at the ordinary physical level, even if you ignore all higher considerations. For example, what guarantee is there that you will always be happy? What do you do when there is death, which is certain even for the materialists. Just ignore it? Pretend it does not happen? The body is the only reality for them, which is subject to disease and injury even before its end.

"Again, what kind of society can a philosophy like that build? There are bound to be conflicts between one person's happiness and that of another. And then someone has got to work. Right? What solutions does it offer? If its followers deny the existence of the spirit, they have to replace it with something else positive. They have nothing of that sort. They just didn't think enough about it. Thus Cārvāka's materialism is both selfish and utterly naïve. No thinking person cares to take a second look at it."

This had indeed been a long session and we had to adjourn reluctantly for our evening rites.

31
THE END AS BEGINNING

The Ācārya achieved the highest glory in all fields, an achievement unthinkable for ordinary mortals. He was a child prodigy, performed rituals as a *brahmacārin*, accepted *sannyāsa* at the age of eight, wrote commentaries on all major works of *advaita*, toured the length and breadth of the country more than once, vanquished all opposing sects, and established the supremacy of the unitary consciousness which is the everlasting foundation of all existence. Claiming the throne of omniscience was his latest triumphal act. It was at our urging that he did it, more as a vindication of his doctrines than for personal glory.

The Ācārya suggested that we leave Kāshmīr and move southward. He asked most of his disciples to go to Śṛṅgerī. A few including me were to follow him to Badarī. At Badarī he taught his commentaries to all those who cared to learn, providing unfailing spiritual consolation to householder and *sannyāsin* alike. He was accessible to all people at all times. His patience and his courtesy were proverbial, his compassion overflowing. He was constantly engaged in teaching or meditation and was supremely content with himself. He wanted nothing more. He did not even want the fame. It was incidental to his accomplishments. His only desire and ambition throughout his life had been to make each and every human being see the Almighty in himself and in everyone else, everything else, everywhere else. He remained completely unruffled, unattached. Joy could not elate him nor sorrow sadden. Heat did not bother him, and neither did cold. The world was a shadow of itself. What I could never understand, though, was how he could at the same time treat us all with the tenderness of a mother. He must have simultaneously dwelt in two states of consciousness. At age 32, he was the world's maturest man.

Even as we were just beginning to settle down in Badarī, the Ācārya suddenly announced one morning that we were moving to Kedārnāth, a short distance away. Kedārnāth is a place dedicated to Lord Śiva. Situated at the foot of the Himālayas, it has an unsurpassed natural grandeur. The cold, however was too much for the barely clad *sannyāsins*. Noticing this, the Ācārya prayed to Śiva placing his head at the Lord's feet, and lo, there appeared between the two feet a geyser of hot water to relieve their discomfort. This spring still shields pilgrims from the rigors of the Himālayan cold. He always looked to our every need while he desired nothing in return. Whatever personal service we rendered him was for our satisfaction and not because he wanted it.

On the third day after we arrived in Kedārnāth, the Ācārya summoned all of us to a meeting. He addressed us in a particularly affectionate voice, his face reflecting an unearthly charm. His words were memorable. "Dear friends, I have something to tell you. Please listen carefully, and do not be disturbed by its import. You know that during the many years of our association, we have accomplished many things together. We have traveled together, observed the practices of the people, and helped them reform themselves where they went wrong. We faced many difficulties and dangers together. We also studied together and discovered the basic identity of all beings. We know for a fact that the world is an illusion, that *Brahman* is the Reality, and that the *ātman* in each of us is none other than *Brahman*. This is the essence of all knowledge. This realization is the goal of our life.

"Yet I am aware that as humans we are weak at times. We fail to apply our learning in practice and see things for what they are. I hope that our long discussions have helped you get over this difficulty. The difficulty, as you know, is caused by ignorance. Knowledge is its antidote. The particular ignorance I want you to recall is the notion that this body is permanent. You remember the Yakṣa's question to Dharmarāja in the *Mahābhārata,* 'What is the strangest thing in the world?' and Dharmarāja's answer, 'Everyone knows that one who is born will die some day and sees people dying around him every day, yet he thinks that somehow he is immortal.'"

We did not know what he was driving at until the shocking news came out shortly. "Now prepare yourselves to propagate the wisdom of our teachings on your own. I have taught you all I know and there is very little to *teach*, anyway. You just *know*, just as in the realm of consciousness you don't *do* anything, you just *are*. I have accomplished the task entrusted to me by Lord Śiva and Vyāsa. There is nothing more for me to do in this body. At sunset, you will see this body no more."

There was utter silence in the group as the news sank in. We never thought there would come a day when we would be without our beloved Ācārya. *Vedāntins* though we were, our grief knew no bounds. We were inconsolable as we wept and made desperate pleas to him not to leave us yet. There was nothing impossible for him who could control the mighty Narmadā, who could invoke gods and goddesses, who realized *Brahman.* He spoke again, a bewitching smile on his lips. "Just think of your strange logic. Does a knower of *Brahman* care at all for his fragile body composed of the five gross elements? It is true that the time has come for my body to fall. But where am I going? I am with you all the time. I am in you. Around you. There was no time when I wasn't and at no time will I not be. Only the illusion of the body will disappear. Do you have any questions to ask at this time?"

We were too dumbfounded to speak. Then someone slowly asked in a voice choked with tears, "O Great Soul, kindly let us know the one sure means of right knowledge for ordinary mortals which will lead them to liberation."

The Ācārya referred him to the ten verses that he composed when his was eight years old in answer to his guru Govindapāda's question "Who are you?" He elaborated that the best way to approach the non-dual reality was through a negation of what is unreal. When everything transient is negated, what is left is the enduring Reality. Every *advaitin* should constantly remind himself of this as his spiritual endeavor.

After a brief pause the Ācārya said thoughtfully. "The Truth that we tried to ascertain and the procedure of worship that we suggested in the various temples will fall into disuse and decay unless we make proper arrangements for their continuance. Also it is not possible for anyone to remain at one place and look after the spiritual instruction of the public throughout our vast country So I suggest that there be four missions in the four corners of the land headed by four ācāryas who will be responsible for the well-being of the people in their respective regions. I want you to note that one's physical well-being comes before one's philosophy and dharma. Therefore, these four ācāryas must by all means ensure that even the lowliest peasant in the land is happy. They should intercede with the chiefs of the kingdoms on behalf of these people. It is only then that you can accomplish any higher goals.

"I have often said that this body is contemptible, but it is still our only support and has to be attended to as long as we have not transcended its limitations. No amount of philosophizing will do any good while the body's demands are not met. The paradox therefore is that you must function within the body and at the same time ignore it. You must use your mind in order to annihilate it in the quest for the Self. You should be within your family, yet be aware of its illusory nature. Until you cease to be born, the family is the sole means of begetting legitimate offspring. Some of these will be mahātmās. The family has enough checks within itself to ensure the orderly growth of the society, as laid down in the *Gṛhya Sūtra*. Not everyone can or need be a *sannyāsin*. Taming the beast in man and encouraging the human in him will help him in the discovery of himself. Then the world will be peopled by liberated individuals. Let a spirit of inquiry guide such a revolution on earth. Let every man, woman, and child think freely in all spiritual matters. Never impose your own perceptions on others. Remember that the one Reality is apprehended by many in many ways."

Then I made bold to ask what he had in mind regarding the establishment of the missions he referred to. "This is only my suggestion. You can modify it in any way you like. The four centers of spiritual knowledge can be located at Pūrī in the east, Śṛṅgerī in the south, Dvārakā in the west, and Jyotirdhāma in the north. And, if I may make a further suggestion, you, Sureśvara, Hastāmalaka, and Toṭaka be the first chiefs of these centers." He looked at us for comments. We had none. We were still too dazed to realize what was happening. He then dictated to King Sudhanvan the procedures for the administration of these missions. This detailed book of rules came to be known as *Mahānuśāsana*.

The Ācārya then rested against the trunk of the *bilva* tree behind him for a minute with half-closed eyes. Slowly he began to speak. "Really there is nothing more for me to say. I would like to thank all of you who have rendered so much personal service to me. Padmapāda twice saved my life. Toṭaka cheerfully washed my clothes, made arrangements for the daily rites, and respected my every wish as a command. Everyone else has helped me in a thousand imperceptible ways over the years. I am grateful to you all. May you all enjoy the bliss of *Brahman* eternally."

I could not check my tears at this expression of gratitude There was nothing that anyone of us did for the Ācārya that he could not have done himself. And what about everything that *he* did for us? Where would I or Toṭaka be today but for his grace and limitless compassion? How can we ever thank him for that?

Looking at no one in particular, the Ācārya then continued. "Lord, I humbly beg your forgiveness for three transgressions that I have committed: I knew you were omnipresent, yet I made pilgrimages to various temples. I knew you were beyond mind, yet I meditated on you with my mind. I knew you were beyond speech, yet I composed verses in your praise. When you and I are one and the same, how could I ever do any of these things? There is no difference, no difference at all. There is just the One, no second."

The sun was about to disappear in the beyond. The Ācārya looked steadily at it for a few minutes and said almost cheerfully, "Now, let's all chant the primordial syllable followed by the eternal utterances:

Om prajñānam brahma
Om ayamātmā brahma
Om tat tvam asi
Om aham brahmāsmi

When we were chanting the last declaration, the Ācārya's face brightened. He joined us in an especially resonant voice:

aham brahmāsmi
aham brahmāsmi
aham brahmāsmi

When the chorus was at its peak, there was a flood of light all around us and we were lulled into a feeling of supernal joy. When we came to shortly, we just saw the *bilva* tree. The light was gone.

EPILOGUE

I met the Ācārya when he was twelve, and lived with him for two decades.

Now, life is not the same without him.

I know that I must not have any longing for any person, place, or object. But he was not *any* person. He was my *Ācārya*.

He spoke and his word was God. And he was the word. And the word was Silence.

The Ācārya is silent. Praise be to the Ācārya!

A MILLENNIAL MEDITATION*

I am born in this body
through a dark and dreary passage
groping into a world already in the dark.
I see the scene on the screen.
I cry I feed I sleep,
I forget the screen.
Now my mother then my father
fill the screen.
I talk I walk I crawl the vast expanse of my crib,
and chatter till I am fed, again,
secure under the blanket.
Darkness is so comforting.

I learn the language, the idiom of the world,
feeling my way through the jungle of notions
and sentiments.
I study the Vedas, the sastras, *the* puranas,
and the classics, grammar, logic,
and philosophy. Relentless words
labyrinthine that shroud the Reality.

I see my body. I like it. I love it.
I take care of it, as it crumbles
right under my nose.
I wash it, aromatize it, decorate it,
as the winds wither it.

I look around and like what I see,
I smell the flowers,
and watch the rainbow melt
into the liquid sky.

Reprinted by kind permission from *The Mountain Path* (Tiruvannamalai: Ramanasramam) Aradhana issue, 2000.

The sun smiles, the rains drench, the stars shine
and the seas moan in utter ecstasy.

NOT HAPPY

The mind churns, the heart races.
I like some things, hate others.
Feelings, fears, emotions, desires,
strange modifications of the mind
that haven't been there before.
I seek pleasure, shun pain.
I make friends, feel the pangs of flesh.
I indulge. It is all so real.
Passion guides and instinct rules.
I see the scene, the screen is blurred.

I work, work to live, live to eat,
and eat to indulge.
The body takes charge and controls the mind.
I work, I rest, I win, I lose.
I get me a partner, a helpmate,
to double my rapture,
to have all I want and more.
I pursue more happiness working harder
making more and spending more,
aiming to suck up all the pleasures of the world
in one giant gulp.

I sing I dance I write,
I scale the heights of art into
an emptiness most empty.
I build forts and mansions,

I dare the mysteries of the skies
and dive into oceans to steal their secrets.
I probe the laws of nature,
I distil the alchemy of the elements
and unravel the implicit formulae of existence.
I peer countless miles into space
seeking the alleged Creator.
Having found none,
I feel that I am greater than He or She
as the case may be.

STILL NOT HAPPY

Miracles do not a seer make,
when he fails to see his own mistake.

I have many a brother and sister,
aunts and uncles,
and children and children's children,
manservants and maids to please.
But I am alone at night, though consorted,
for reasons beyond explanation.
What is company that is least companionable?
Who is company for one who remains most alone?
And the children get sick and the old-timers drop,
and sometimes the young ones, too.
The heart aches and the mind follows suit.
The mind agitated, agitates the spirit.

The arts evanesce and the sciences cease
and the literatures languish
though I still am,

breathing through a thousand noses
eating through a thousand mouths
and merging in a thousand minds.
I give up, I care no more.
I do and not do the things I do,
I give up the fruits of my labor
so others may gain, I give up
my stake in the action
and gain relief beyond satisfaction.
The end-all is the new be-all.

The fog clears and heart stops
and I can see where I've been
and where I need to be,
where it's really Real.

I think I am dead.
The limbs do not move, the senses do not sense,
the organs do not act.
Darkness ensues presently.
I look within me and take note of it all.
Nothing matters now.
I finally gain control over it all,
more alive than when I was alive,
now that I am dead to the outer world.

I dive into the core of my being
where I disappear to be for all eternity
and beyond. I feel
nothing see nothing hear nothing.

I JUST AM

conscious, blissful, higher than the transient worlds
and the ephemeral gods.
Fire doesn't burn me nor winds dry
seas don't drown me nor weapons hurt,
I am when I don't think that I am,
when I don't know that I am.

My questions cease my quest's done,
my doubts vanish, leaving answers
clear as crystal.
No darkness lingers in Superior Light,
no questions rise in Superior Knowledge,
the knowledge that I am I and no other,
that I alone exist and no other,
I am all, all is me.
I create all in the nooks
of my mind which therefore
cease when the mind ceases, and I remain forever.
Time is but a shadow of the mind
as is space which
ceases when the periphery
is consumed by the center.

The world is only a wink away,
but wholly separated by that wink
for one whose winks destroy it
and establish the Self instead.
Such a one is the master of the world,
its mighty creator and destroyer-at-will.
The world is an idea? Whose?
The world is a thought? Who thought it up?
It's leela? *Sport for whom?*

First, I am.
Not the I that was born,
but the I that's always been.
I am, *therefore I think I act I speak.*
And, after I have thought enough
and spoken enough and acted enough,
I still am,
happy without seeking to be,
and blissful without trying to be.
There is no choice but to be
in the Perennial Present,
the Pure Consciousness
unchanging and unchangeable,
ageless timeless nameless formless.

INDEX